The New Sobriety

Using Ancient Stoic Wisdom

Sean Easting

losses, direct or indirect, that are incurred as a result of the use of the information contained within this document, including, but not limited to, errors, omissions, or inaccuracies.

Table of Contents

Introduction

One day, as I was browsing the shelves of a nearby bookstore, I discovered a book filled with the insightful parables and teachings of Stoic philosophers. Intrigued by their profound wisdom, I made the decision to give it a chance, completely unaware of the transformative impression it would have on my life.

The Archer and the Target, a parable attributed to Antipater, had a profound impact on me. It resonated deeply as I battled with substance abuse, feeling like every effort towards recovery was in vain.

The parable served as a powerful reminder to set a clear and meaningful goal in my journey to sobriety, akin to an archer aiming for the bullseye. It emphasized focusing on what I could control—my thoughts, actions, and choices. This realization became my guiding light, propelling me forward with steady progress. The parable taught me that success wasn't solely determined by hitting the target; it was about the careful aim and mindful shooting of the arrow. While I aimed for the mark, I understood that the final result wasn't entirely in my hands. What truly mattered was giving my utmost care, dedication, and mindfulness to the pursuit of my goal.

By embracing this wisdom, I set off on my path to sobriety with a renewed sense of determination. The archer's ability to concentrate and stay committed became the guiding principles that propelled me forward in times of temptation and uncertainty. I understood that my success relied on the choices and actions I made each day, ensuring they aligned with my ultimate goal.

Today, driven by my own personal journey of growth, I am committed to assisting others in their own paths towards recovery. I aim to inspire and guide individuals trapped in addiction by sharing the powerful teachings and stories of the Stoic philosophers. By illustrating the transformative power of Stoic principles, my goal is to illuminate the way towards genuine freedom and inner resilience.

If you're struggling to overcome addiction in a world full of distractions and temptations, you may feel like it's an impossible task. However, I assure you that there is hope. This book explores the ancient wisdom of Stoic philosophy and how it can help you break free from addiction and transform your life. Welcome to *The New Sobriety*, where you'll discover the power of Stoicism for lasting sobriety and personal growth. You can liberate yourself from dependency and live a life of purpose, fulfillment, and freedom. This is not a distant dream but a tangible reality within your grasp.

Before we embark on this journey together, let us take a moment to understand your pain, struggles, and aspirations. I recognize that addiction affects individuals from all walks of life, irrespective of the substances or behaviors they are addicted to. Whether it's alcohol, drugs, gambling, or even the addictive allure of social media, the grip of addiction can be suffocating, causing immense pain, despair, and isolation.

I also acknowledge that it is the weight of your pain that has led you here, seeking a remedy, and we want you to know that we truly comprehend. We empathize with the challenges you face, and our purpose is to illuminate the path toward a brighter tomorrow. Within the confines of this book, you will discover not only solace but also a pragmatic framework firmly grounded in Stoic philosophy. It is this framework that can empower you to liberate yourself from the entanglements of addiction and rekindle the profound joy of living.

There are several compelling reasons to use Stoicism as a framework for treating addiction. While traditional approaches often focus on medical treatments or therapy, Stoic philosophy offers a unique perspective that addresses the root causes of addiction and provides practical tools for overcoming it.

By adopting the principles of Stoic philosophy, individuals can develop a new mindset and approach to addiction. They can gain a fresh perspective on their struggles, cultivate resilience, and enhance self-awareness. Stoicism offers practical tools and techniques that empower individuals to take control of their lives, build inner strength, and ultimately achieve lasting sobriety.

In *The New Sobriety*, you will delve deeply into Stoic philosophy and its powerful wisdom on addiction and recovery. The book is designed to take you through a holistic journey of transformation, providing effective tools and exercises that will enable you to overcome addiction and establish a firm basis for long-term sobriety.

Here is a glimpse of what you will learn within these pages:

Chapter 1: Introduction to Stoic Philosophy

Provides a comprehensive overview of Stoic philosophy, including its principles of living in harmony with nature and reason, cultivating virtues, practicing mindfulness, and finding true happiness within oneself. Explores the Stoic approach to death, detachment from material possessions, and serving society. Applies Stoic philosophy to sobriety and addiction recovery.

Chapter 2: Understanding Addiction From a Stoic Perspective

Examines addiction types, causes, and contributing factors, including substance and non-substance addictions. Explores accessibility, environmental influences, genetic predispositions, mental health disorders, and more. Offers insights into the complex interplay between external circumstances and internal disposition for lasting sobriety and personal growth.

Chapter 3: Embracing the Dichotomy of Control

Focuses on distinguishing between what can and cannot be controlled. Explores external factors beyond control, highlights aspects within control, and provides practical ways to apply Stoic principles to recovery. Guides individuals in navigating challenges and fostering personal growth on the path to sobriety.

Chapter 4: Cultivating Resilience Through Adversity

Explores Stoic principles for building mental and emotional resilience while embracing challenges. Covers strategies such as accepting difficult emotions, developing emotional intelligence, cultivating gratitude, and adopting a growth mindset. Emphasizes personal responsibility, self-discipline, and self-awareness in navigating adversity for sobriety and personal growth.

Chapter 5: Practicing Mindfulness and Self-Awareness

Guides readers in identifying triggers, cultivating self-awareness, and embracing mindfulness. Explores trigger responses, self-reflection, observing thoughts and emotions, and practical steps for mindfulness. Helps individuals gain insight into addiction triggers, develop self-awareness, and navigate the journey to sobriety and personal transformation.

Chapter 6: Cultivating Virtue and Personal Growth

Explores Stoic virtues and practices for personal development in addiction recovery. Covers wisdom, courage, temperance, justice, and practices like embracing difficulties, seeking inspiration, practicing gratitude, and prioritizing truth. Fosters personal growth and transformation through the incorporation of these virtues and practices.

Chapter 7: Seeking Reflection Through Wisdom and Learning

Delves into Stoic teachings for enhancing self-understanding and addressing addiction. Covers reflection on personal history, identifying triggers, journaling, seeking support, practicing self-compassion, understanding addiction science, setting goals, mindfulness, self-awareness, support networks, self-care, and commitment to recovery. Guides readers in gaining insight, confronting addiction, and navigating the recovery journey.

Chapter 8: Fostering Emotional Mastery and Detachment

Emphasizes emotional sobriety and provides techniques to cultivate emotional detachment. Addresses emotional issues, managing challenging emotions, and fostering healthier relationships. Explores Stoic techniques such as negative visualization, self-distancing, gratitude practice, and embracing minimalism. Develops emotional regulation, detachment, and acceptance in the recovery journey.

Chapter 9: Building a Supportive Stoic Community

Focuses on establishing connections within the Stoic community and sharing experiences for growth. Explores empathy, kindness, gratitude, humility, social skills, authenticity, vulnerability, forgiveness, patience, and community-building. Emphasizes creating a supportive environment and sharing experiences with purpose. Cultivates a supportive Stoic community and fosters personal and collective growth in sobriety and personal development.

My chance encounter with the parables of the Stoic philosophers has become a pivotal chapter in my life, illuminating the profound impact that timeless wisdom can have on our journey towards healing and personal growth. By the end of this book, you will not only possess a deep understanding of Stoic philosophy and its profound insights into addiction and recovery but you will also be equipped with practical tools and techniques to implement these principles in your own life.

I invite you to embrace *The New Sobriety* and embark on a journey of self-discovery, resilience, and personal transformation. Let the ancient wisdom of Stoicism be your guiding light toward a life of sobriety, fulfillment, and true freedom. Together, we will navigate the challenges and celebrate the victories on this path to lasting sobriety.

Chapter 1:

Introduction to Stoic

Philosophy

In the first chapter, we embark on a captivating journey into the ancient wisdom of Stoicism. We explore its origins, tracing back to Zeno of Citium in ancient Greece, and delve into its central tenet of living in accordance with rationality and natural laws. Stoicism emphasizes focusing on what we can control and letting go of external factors. Cultivating virtues, embracing mindfulness, and recognizing the transient nature of material possessions are key aspects. Stoicism teaches that true happiness comes from within and encourages contributing to society. This chapter also lays the groundwork for applying Stoic philosophy to sobriety and addiction recovery, providing a solid foundation for lasting personal growth.

A Beginner's Guide to Stoicism

Stoicism, a philosophical school that traces its roots back to ancient Greece, was established by Zeno of

Citium around 300 BCE. The ancient Greek Stoics saw themselves as the successors of Socratic ethical philosophy and the natural philosophy of Heraclitus of Ephesus (Garrett, 2021). Born out of a desire to understand the nature of existence and the human condition, Stoicism developed into a comprehensive philosophy that resonates with individuals seeking wisdom, guidance, and tranquility in an unpredictable world.

The Stoics were driven by a desire to unravel the fundamental principles that governed the universe. They firmly believed that the cosmos operated in accordance with rational and natural laws (Camilleri, 2023). With this understanding, they advocated for human beings, as rational beings themselves, to align their lives with these underlying principles. The Stoics saw this alignment as a means to achieve harmony and live in sync with the true essence of the cosmos.

Stoic philosophy centers around recognizing the limited control humans have over their surroundings. According to Stoicism, individuals have the ability to influence only their own thoughts, choices, and actions, whereas external events or the actions of others are considered beyond their control (Camilleri, 2023). By focusing on things that can be controlled and accepting what cannot, Stoics aim to avoid concern, anxiety, and annoyance that are not essential.

For the Stoics, living a virtuous life takes center stage. They firmly hold the belief that genuine fulfillment and happiness are achievable through the development and practice of virtuous qualities, including wisdom, courage, self-control, justice, and kindness (Avalon

Malibu, 2020). By consciously embracing and embodying these virtues, individuals can skillfully navigate the trials and tribulations of life with integrity, while also making meaningful contributions to the overall welfare of society.

Stoicism also encourages adherents to come to terms with the impermanence of life. The inevitability of death and the ever-changing nature of the world are seen as fundamental truths to be acknowledged and embraced (FitMind, 2020). By accepting the transient nature of existence, Stoics seek to find peace and contentment in the present moment, appreciating the fleeting beauty and experiences that life has to offer.

The Stoic philosophy extends beyond material possessions, emphasizing the insignificance of external wealth and success as sources of true happiness (Tosin, 2023a). Stoics advocate for an inner transformation, whereby individuals can find lasting fulfillment through the development of their character and the pursuit of wisdom. They believe that genuine happiness is derived from a sense of self-mastery and inner resilience, independent of external circumstances.

Stoicism has had a profound influence on the philosophies and perspectives of numerous individuals throughout history. The writings of esteemed Stoic philosophers like Marcus Aurelius, Seneca, and Epictetus have enduringly offered invaluable wisdom and counsel to thinkers, leaders, and everyday individuals alike across the ages (Gill, 2019). Their profound understanding of the self, the significance of rationality, and the quest for virtue remain just as pertinent in the present day as they were centuries ago.

These timeless insights continue to inspire and deeply resonate with readers who are on a journey of self-discovery, seeking enlightenment, and striving for personal growth.

Stoic Stories

As mentioned in the introduction, the Stoic philosophers sometimes utilized parables and allegories to convey the principles and values underscoring their philosophy. These stories offer valuable insights into the Stoic mindset, encouraging individuals to focus on what they can control, accept the natural course of events, and cultivate inner tranquility and resilience.

The Stoic in a Storm at Sea According to Gellius (1927)

A group of individuals embarked on a sailing journey from Cassiopa to Brundisium, crossing the vast and stormy Ionian Sea. It was a tough journey right from the start. During the night after their first day at sea, they faced a powerful side-wind that caused their ship to fill with water. They tried their best to fix the problem, but the danger seemed to stick around.

As the sun finally rose on the following day, the storm didn't let up. In fact, it got worse with frequent whirlwinds, a dark sky, thick fog, and scary-looking cloud formations called typhoons. One of the passengers on this adventurous trip was a well-known philosopher from the Stoic group. He was someone respected for his wisdom back in Athens. Curious about how he was coping with the terrifying situation, a fellow traveler checked on him.

Surprisingly, the philosopher looked frightened and pale, though he was trying not to show it outwardly like the rest. As the storm eventually settled and the sea calmed down, a well-off Greek passenger approached the philosopher with a playful tone. He teased the philosopher, asking why he was scared while the wealthy man himself hadn't shown any fear.

After a moment's hesitation, the philosopher explained, drawing on the words of another wise person named Aristippus. He pointed out that their motives were different—the rich man need not worry much about his life since he lived a carefree lifestyle. On the other hand, the philosopher was concerned about someone more important, an Aristippus.

As they approached their destination with peaceful waters and skies, the curious traveler asked the philosopher why he was initially afraid, which he had kept to himself earlier. The philosopher referred to the teachings of the famous philosopher named Epictetus. He shared a simple idea that makes sense to all of us: when something scary or dangerous suddenly happens, it's natural for anyone, even a wise person, to feel scared for a brief moment. It's like our minds and bodies react automatically.

However, the difference between a wise person and someone else lies in how they handle it. Someone who is less wise might believe the scary thoughts and let them control their feelings, but a wise person recognizes these thoughts for what they are—just fleeting and unfounded fears.

So, the lesson here is that it's natural for all of us to feel afraid sometimes, but we shouldn't let those fears take over our thoughts. Instead, we can remind ourselves that they are just passing thoughts, and we'll be able to handle the situation with courage and strength.

Epictetus' Metaphors

Epictetus masterfully employs a plethora of vivid metaphors to paint a comprehensive picture of the ideal Stoic attitude towards life. Drawing from the depths of his philosophical wisdom, he skillfully weaves these analogies to illuminate profound insights and guide his followers on their journey to inner tranquility and virtuous living (Seddon, n.d.).

Life as a Festival

In one analogy, life is likened to a festival, orchestrated for our benefit by the divine. With this perspective, we are encouraged to embrace life's hardships with equanimity, keeping our focus on the larger spectacle unfolding before us. As mortals on this earth, we are partaking in a brief but meaningful pageant within the grand design of the universe.

Stoic ethics, according to Epictetus, urges us to actively contribute to this festival of life by living well and fulfilling our duties as compassionate and sociable citizens in the universal city governed by the divine order.

Life as a Game

In another metaphor, life is compared to a game of dice or a ball game. Just as the value of dice and counters lies not in themselves but in how skillfully the game is played, external things in life are indifferent; what truly matters is how we navigate and respond to them. Stoicism teaches us to develop our faculties of dexterity, good judgment, and wisdom, thus enabling us to play well in the game of life.

The philosopher extends the metaphor of games to discussions of suicide, advocating that if life becomes unbearable, we can choose to depart from it like a player leaving a game that no longer amuses them.

Life as Weaving

Epictetus also likens life to weaving, where we are presented with various materials that we must skillfully use to create the best outcomes possible. Just as a weaver creates beautiful cloth from the wool, we must make the most of the circumstances and materials that come our way, fulfilling our duties and living virtuously.

Life as a Play

Drawing from the metaphor of life as a play, Epictetus highlights the importance of recognizing our roles and accepting our fate. While we may aim for certain roles, the ultimate casting is beyond our control. Like actors in a play, we must excel in the roles assigned to us, using our talents and virtues to act well in the cosmic drama.

Life as an Athletic Contest

Epictetus also invites us to view our training in Stoic ethics as akin to an athlete's preparation for a contest. Just as an athlete diligently trains before entering the arena, our philosophical training prepares us for a life aligned with Stoic ideals. Epictetus urges us not to delay, for the challenges and opportunities of life await us, demanding that we live fully as mature individuals making progress toward virtue.

Life as Military Service

Life is compared to military service, with the understanding that we all serve under the divine command. Each person's life represents a soldier's campaign, filled with diverse challenges and responsibilities. Embracing our role as soldiers, we must fulfill our duties as directed by the universal commander, contributing to the greater order and well-being of the cosmic army.

Marcus Aurelius

Marcus Aurelius beautifully contrasts the temporary nature of the physical body with the fleeting essence of the soul. Life is portrayed as a constant battle and a temporary journey. Amidst life's changes, philosophy stands as the guiding light, offering direction and wisdom.

> "In simple terms, everything related to our physical body is like a flowing stream, constantly changing and temporary. On the other hand, what pertains to our inner self, our soul, is like a fleeting dream or vapor. Life is described as a constant battle and a temporary stay in a foreign land, and any fame or recognition we may receive will eventually be forgotten.
>
> So, what can guide a person through this ever-changing journey of life? The answer is philosophy, the one and only thing that can provide direction and wisdom." (Aurelius, 2017a)

Seneca (n.d.)

Seneca greets his friend Lucilius and recounts an adventurous sea journey he recently experienced. Despite the calm weather initially, the voyage took a turn for the worse as a storm approached, and Seneca's seasickness became unbearable. He reflects on how we often ignore our bodily ailments until they become too evident to ignore. Seneca compares this to the diseases of the soul, which we may overlook when they are severe. He emphasizes the importance of self-awareness and confessing our faults as a sign of a sound mind.

Seneca encourages Lucilius to devote himself wholly to philosophy, for it has the power to awaken and shake us from our slumber. He urges Lucilius to prioritize philosophy over other distractions, just as one would prioritize recovering from an illness. Philosophy demands daily practice and commitment, offering a life of tranquility and wisdom. By embracing philosophy, one can transcend the limitations of mortals and even rival the gods in wisdom and serenity.

Seneca bids farewell, leaving Lucilius with a parting message to embrace philosophy and let it guide him towards a more enlightened and fulfilled life.

Stoicism Applied to Sobriety and Addiction Recovery

When applied to the context of sobriety and addiction recovery, Stoicism offers practical tools and perspectives that can support individuals on their journey. By embracing the Stoic principles of self-control, acceptance, and virtuous living, those in recovery can develop resilience, find meaning in their experiences, and regain a sense of agency over their lives. It provides a framework for facing challenges, cultivating inner strength, and embracing a mindset that fosters personal growth and well-being.

The parable of The Stoic in a Storm at Sea from Gellius emphasizes that the journey to sobriety and addiction recovery can be a turbulent one, filled with moments of doubt and fear. It acknowledges that everyone, including those with knowledge and experience, can feel vulnerable during the process. However, it also highlights the importance of understanding and embracing those feelings while maintaining the determination to move forward with courage and strength. The story encourages those in recovery to trust in themselves, seek support, and remain steadfast in their commitment to a healthier and addiction-free life.

By using metaphors to compare life to a festival, a game, weaving, a play, an athletic contest, and military service, Epictetus offers profound insights and guidance for those seeking healing and inner tranquility in their battle against addiction. Embracing these perspectives can empower individuals on their path to recovery.

In the context of addiction and recovery, Marcus Aurelius contrasts the transient nature of the physical body with the fleeting essence of the soul. Recovery becomes a constant battle, like a temporary journey in a foreign land. Amidst life's changes, philosophy acts as a guiding light, offering direction and wisdom to navigate this transformative journey.

Seneca's analogy of the sea journey also offers valuable insights. Addiction may start with a sense of calm, but soon becomes turbulent like a stormy sea. Recovery requires courage to confront challenges, just as Seneca chose to head for the shore despite dangers. Embracing philosophy as guidance enables self-awareness and coping strategies, acting as a shield against relapses. Seneca's wisdom encourages individuals to face their struggles with determination and embrace inner growth on the path to healing.

Stoic philosophy is not merely an intellectual pursuit reserved for the wealthy or powerful—it can be a valuable tool for those seeking to navigate addiction recovery (Vecchiola, 2022a). By embracing Stoicism as a way of life, individuals can find the guidance, support, and inspiration they need to overcome their addiction and rebuild their lives in a positive, fulfilling way. This philosophy encourages individuals to focus on what they can control, accept what they cannot, and stay committed to their goals even when faced with difficult obstacles or setbacks.

Stoicism offers valuable insights and techniques to help individuals attain a balanced and moderate lifestyle. Interestingly, many Stoic virtues align with the core principles of substance abuse therapies (Avalon Malibu, 2020). For instance, Stoic concepts such as acceptance, mindfulness, and self-control are integral components of many substance abuse treatment modalities. By incorporating Stoic teachings into addiction recovery programs, individuals can learn to manage their thoughts, emotions, and behaviors more effectively, promoting positive, lasting change.

Nine Principles of Stoic Philosophy

Stoic philosophy offers a practical and insightful framework for living a fulfilling and balanced life. By embracing these nine principles, we can cultivate wisdom, resilience, and inner peace, guiding us toward a life of purpose and contentment. They will also be explored more deeply in further chapters.

Embrace Natural and Rational Living

Living according to nature and reason entails aligning our actions and choices with the principles of the natural world and rational thinking. By doing so, we can lead a more balanced and fulfilling life. This means recognizing the interconnectedness of all things and striving to live in harmony with the natural order.

Nurture Virtues: Wisdom, Courage, Justice, Self-Control

The concept of Stoic virtue differs greatly from the modern understanding of the term (Irvine, 2009). Cultivating the virtues of wisdom, courage, justice, and self-control are essential for personal growth and ethical living. Wisdom enables us to make informed decisions, while courage gives us the strength to face challenges and overcome obstacles. Justice ensures fairness and equality in our interactions, and self-control helps us regulate our impulses and desires.

Embrace Control: Accept the Uncontrollable

Focusing on what is within our control and accepting what is not is a core principle we will name the Dichotomy of Control. By directing our energy towards things we can influence, such as our thoughts, actions, and attitudes, we can find a sense of empowerment and avoid unnecessary distress caused by fixating on external factors beyond our control.

Embrace the Present: Release the Past, Unburden the Future

Living in the present moment is required to find contentment and peace. Dwelling on the past or worrying about the future only detracts from our ability to fully experience and appreciate the present. By practicing mindfulness and being fully present in each moment, we can enhance our overall well-being and find joy in the simple pleasures of life.

Let Go of Material Attachments

Not being attached to material possessions involves recognizing that true happiness does not come from accumulating material wealth. While material possessions can provide temporary satisfaction, they do not bring lasting fulfillment. By cultivating detachment from material possessions, we can free ourselves from the constant desire for more and find contentment in the present moment.

Think about a person who has lost everything and now possesses only a loincloth (Irvine, 2009). The Stoics suggest that even in such dire circumstances, it could still get worse–he could lose the loincloth as well. This thought prompts reflection on his situation. Now, let's imagine that he does lose the loincloth. Despite this, if he still maintains good health, his circumstances could be even worse than before, which is something he should acknowledge. And if his health further deteriorates, he can still be grateful for being alive despite all the hardships.

Embrace Life's Transience

Embracing the inevitability of death and the impermanence of life is an important aspect of living a meaningful life. Recognizing that life is transient and finite can motivate us to make the most of our time and prioritize what truly matters. It encourages us to live authentically, cherish relationships, and pursue our passions without delay.

Internal Happiness: Independent of External Factors

Recognizing that happiness originates from within and is not solely reliant on external circumstances is a profound realization. While external factors like wealth, success, or social status may provide temporary joy, true and enduring happiness is cultivated through inner peace, gratitude, and contentment. It involves nurturing positive emotions, prioritizing self-care, and dedicating oneself to personal growth and fulfillment. By embracing this understanding, we can unlock the key to a fulfilling and meaningful life, regardless of the external circumstances we encounter.

Contribute to the Common Good

Engaging in activities that benefit society as a whole is an integral part of leading a meaningful and satisfying life. When we utilize our unique abilities, expertise, and resources to bring about positive changes in the lives of others and the world at large, we can experience a profound sense of purpose and contentment. Whether it is through simple acts of kindness, dedicating our time to volunteer work, or pursuing a career that has a positive societal impact, our contributions help us forge a deeper connection and sense of belonging within society.

Stay Calm and Rational Amid Challenges

Maintaining a calm and rational mindset in the face of challenges and adversity is a principle Stoicism is known for. By cultivating resilience and practicing emotional regulation, we can navigate difficult circumstances with composure and clarity. Instead of being consumed by negative emotions or reacting impulsively, a calm and rational mindset allows us to respond thoughtfully and effectively to challenges, find solutions, and learn from adversity.

Conclusion

The first chapter introduced Stoicism, an ancient philosophy that aligns human lives with the rationality of the universe. Stoicism can be applied to sobriety and addiction recovery, emphasizing acceptance, mindfulness, and self-control. By embracing Stoic principles, we find contentment, inner peace, and appreciation for life's fleeting moments. Genuine happiness comes from within, contributing to the greater good, and maintaining a rational mindset in challenges. These principles provide a framework for a virtuous and fulfilling life, relevant to sobriety and overall well-being.

Chapter 2:

Understanding Addiction

from a Stoic Perspective

In this chapter, we delve into addiction from a Stoic perspective, exploring its types, causes, and strategies for overcoming it. We examine both substance and non-substance addictions, offering a comprehensive understanding of addictive behaviors. By exploring influences like accessibility, environment, genetics, mental health, and stress, we gain insight into the complexity of addiction. Stoic philosophy emphasizes personal agency, and we explore how individuals can tap into their inner strength and make conscious choices aligned with their values. Practical strategies rooted in Stoic philosophy, such as self-discipline, mindfulness, reframing perceptions, and pursuing virtue, are provided to support the journey of recovery.

Exploring Addiction Through the Lens of Stoic Philosophy

There is often a lack of understanding surrounding why some people become addicted to substances or behaviors. It is a common misconception to believe that they are morally weak or lack willpower and that they could easily stop using by making a simple choice. In truth, addiction is a multifaceted disease, and overcoming it typically requires more than just good intentions or strong determination. Addictions alter the brain in ways that make quitting a challenging endeavor, even for individuals who genuinely desire to quit. Fortunately, extensive research has shed light on how drugs impact the brain, leading to the development of treatments that can aid individuals in recovering from addiction and living fulfilling and productive lives (National Institute on Drug Abuse, 2018).

Stoic philosophy holds valuable teachings and wisdom that can revolutionize our understanding and approach to addiction recovery. By adopting these principles, individuals can gain a new perspective, and develop important skills and mindsets that foster lasting transformation. This is why Stoicism is considered highly effective in addiction treatment.

Stoicism offers a profound understanding that sheds light on its roots in our attachments to external things and our cravings for pleasure or avoidance of pain. Through this philosophy, we are encouraged to explore our attachments and desires, which allows us to uncover the deeper causes behind addictive behaviors. This insightful process paves the way for self-discovery and empowers us to address addiction at its core.

Types of Addiction

Addiction is a chronic and persistent condition characterized by an individual's irresistible urge to seek and engage in substance use or specific activities, despite negative consequences (Cleveland Clinic, 2023). It can take various forms, including both substance and non-substance addiction. Substance addiction typically refers to the compulsive use and abuse of drugs or alcohol, while non-substance addiction, also known as behavioral addiction, involves compulsive engagement in specific behaviors or activities. Substances encompass drugs that have addictive properties, while behavioral addictions can arise from any activity that stimulates the brain's reward system. Understanding the distinctions and similarities between these two types is crucial for effective recognition, intervention, and treatment.

Substance Addiction

- alcohol

- anti-anxiety drugs

- caffeine

- cannabis (marijuana)

- hallucinogens

- inhalants

- tobacco

Non-Substance Addiction

- dieting

- overeating

- exercising

- gambling

- having Sex

- shoplifting

- shopping

- video gaming

- viewing pornography

Causes of Addiction

Addiction is a disease that arises from various underlying factors. These factors, including trauma, mental health issues, and genetics, are strongly associated with addiction but are not always the direct cause (The Phoenix Recovery Center, 2020). Nevertheless, they can increase the probability of developing an addiction after substance abuse.

Accessibility

Accessibility to drugs or alcohol is a leading factor in determining the risk of addiction to them—when these substances are easily accessible, the likelihood of developing an addiction increases. The availability of these substances or behaviors creates a challenging environment where resisting temptation and avoiding triggers becomes more difficult. Stoic philosophy teaches individuals to focus on what they can control, cultivating inner strength and resilience to navigate the challenges posed despite accessibility.

Environmental Factors

Environmental factors play a powerful role in addiction. Early exposure increases the likelihood of addiction later in life, and childhood trauma or abuse also contributes to the risk of addiction. Poor social support, such as isolation and loneliness, further increases vulnerability. Recognizing these environmental factors is crucial in addressing the root causes of addiction. Stoicism emphasizes resilience and self-control in the face of adversity, helping individuals navigate such environmental challenges and thus reduce their susceptibility to addiction.

Genetic Factors

Genetic variations can make individuals more susceptible to addiction by influencing how the brain responds to drugs, alcohol, or addictive behaviors. A family history of addiction also increases the likelihood of developing addictive tendencies. Understanding these genetic factors provides insights into the complex interplay between biology and addiction. Stoic concepts encourage individuals to focus on what they can control, adopt healthy coping mechanisms, and make informed choices to mitigate the risk of addiction.

Lack of Purpose

A lack of purpose or direction in life can lead individuals to seek temporary relief or excitement through drugs or alcohol. Addiction can develop as individuals try to fill a void or find meaning through substance use. Stoicism teaches individuals to find purpose from within, cultivating self-reflection, and aligning actions with personal values. By breaking free from the pursuit of substances as a source of purpose, individuals can overcome addiction and lead fulfilling lives.

Mental Health Disorders

Mental health disorders such as anxiety, depression, or ADHD increase the risk of addiction. Substance use may be done as a form of self-medication, worsening underlying mental health conditions. Addiction can exacerbate mental health symptoms, creating a vicious cycle. Stoic philosophy encourages individuals to develop resilience, self-awareness, and emotional well-being. By practicing Stoic principles, individuals can address mental health challenges without relying on addictive substances. Some challenges will always require the assistance of a trained medical professional.

Peer Pressure

Peer pressure significantly influences the development of addiction, particularly during adolescence and young adulthood. Individuals may succumb to substance use to fit in with social groups and avoid feeling left out. The normalization of substance use within one's social environment increases the risk of addiction. Stoic concepts help individuals resist these external pressures, focus on personal values, and develop inner strength to make choices aligned with their long-term well-being and goals.

Poor Impulse Control

Poor impulse control makes it challenging to resist the immediate pleasure or relief provided by drugs or alcohol. Addiction can develop as a result of impulsive behavior. Stoicism emphasizes self-discipline, reflection, and considering long-term consequences. By practicing Stoic principles, individuals can strengthen their impulse control and make choices that align with their values and well-being.

Sensation-Seeking

Sensation-seekers, who enjoy taking risks and seeking intense experiences, are more susceptible to addiction. The pleasure and excitement induced by drugs or alcohol appeal to their nature. Stoic philosophy encourages individuals to find contentment within themselves, reducing the need for external stimuli. By cultivating mindfulness and self-control, individuals can manage sensation-seeking tendencies and find fulfillment in healthier ways.

According to the Stoics, it is essential to occasionally refrain from seeking pleasure. They caution that pleasure has a negative aspect; pursuing it is akin to chasing a wild beast that can harm us once captured. Seneca also compares intense pleasures to captors—the more pleasures one pursues, the more they become our masters, dictating our actions and enslaving us (Irvine, 2009).

Stress and Trauma

Stressful life events or traumatic experiences can lead individuals to turn to drugs, alcohol, or other coping mechanisms. Addiction may develop as a way of self-medicating difficult emotions or experiences. Stoicism teaches us to develop resilience and adaptability in the face of adversity. By practicing acceptance and focusing on what is within their control, individuals can better manage stress and trauma, reducing their reliance on addictive substances.

External Factors vs. Internal Disposition

Addiction can be influenced by both external factors and internal disposition. External factors refer to the environmental and social circumstances that contribute to the development and maintenance of addiction, while internal disposition pertains to individual characteristics and traits that make some individuals more susceptible to addiction than others. Understanding the interplay between these two aspects is crucial in comprehending the complexity of addiction.

External factors can include the availability and accessibility of addictive substances, peer pressure, societal norms, family dynamics, and exposure to stressors or traumatic events. The presence of addictive substances, such as drugs, alcohol, pornography or gambling increases the likelihood of developing an addiction. For example, living in a neighborhood with a high prevalence of drug use or having easy access to alcohol in a household can heighten the risk of substance abuse and addiction.

Social influences are also an external factor contributing to addiction. Peer pressure and the desire to fit in can lead individuals to experiment with drugs or engage in addictive behaviors. Additionally, societal norms and cultural acceptance of substance use can influence an individual's likelihood of developing an addiction. Family dynamics, including parental substance abuse or dysfunctional relationships, can also contribute to the development of addictive behaviors in individuals.

Internal disposition, on the other hand, involves individual characteristics and traits that can predispose someone to addiction. These factors may include genetic predisposition, personality traits, mental health conditions, and coping mechanisms. Genetic factors can influence an individual's vulnerability to addiction by affecting their brain chemistry and response to substances. Some individuals may possess genetic variations that make them more or less susceptible to the addictive effects of certain substances.

Personality traits such as impulsivity, sensation-seeking, and low self-esteem, can increase the likelihood of developing addictions. Individuals with certain mental health conditions, such as depression, anxiety, or trauma-related disorders, may turn to substances as a form of self-medication or escape from their emotional pain. Moreover, ineffective coping mechanisms, such as using drugs or engaging in addictive behaviors as a way to cope with stress or emotional difficulties, can contribute to the development of addiction.

While external factors can create an environment conducive to addiction, an individual's internal disposition determines their susceptibility and response to these factors. Not everyone exposed to the same external influences will develop an addiction, highlighting the significance of internal factors.

Conclusion

This chapter explored addiction through a Stoic lens, offering insights and strategies for overcoming it. Stoicism emphasizes personal agency and the power of choices in addiction recovery. By focusing on what is within our control and aligning our actions with virtuous principles, we can develop resilience and break free from addiction's hold. Understanding addiction from a Stoic perspective provides a transformative path to recovery, fostering self-awareness and self-discipline. By embracing Stoic principles, we can find inner tranquility and lead lives driven by reason, virtue, and personal growth.

Chapter 3:

Embracing the Dichotomy

of Control

In this chapter, we explore the impact of Stoic philosophy on the journey to sobriety and addiction recovery. The Dichotomy of Control is a core principle that guides us in distinguishing between what we can and cannot control. By understanding this concept, we gain insights into navigating addiction by focusing on what we can change and accepting what is beyond our control.

We discuss two key areas: things outside our control and things within our control. Stoicism advises us to let go of futile attempts to control external factors like death, genetics, and the actions of others. Instead, we focus on aspects we can control, such as our actions, emotions, habits, relationships, and personal growth. By directing our efforts towards these areas, we gain agency over our lives and make meaningful changes on the path to sobriety.

Epictetus offers unconventional advice that challenges the typical approach to finding contentment. While most people believe they must work to fulfill desires and change the world to gain happiness, Epictetus flips this logic. He points out that true happiness cannot be achieved by yearning for what is not present. Instead, he suggests a different strategy: focus on wanting only those things that are easily attainable, ideally seeking only those things you can be certain of obtaining.

Unlike the common pursuit of changing external circumstances, Epictetus advises us to find contentment by changing ourselves, specifically our desires (Irvine, 2009). This advice aligns with the teachings of various philosophers and religious thinkers who have examined human desire and dissatisfaction. They all agree that seeking contentment is more feasible and effective when we adjust our desires and wants, rather than trying to reshape the world around us.

The Dual Nature of Control

Epictetus, the renowned Stoic philosopher, was born into slavery in ancient Greece. Despite this disadvantaged position, he had the opportunity to study Stoic philosophy under the guidance of the philosopher Masunius Rufus (Weaver, 2022). At the age of around 18, Epictetus gained his freedom, coinciding with the passing of Emperor Nero.

Following his newfound liberty, Epictetus journeyed to Rome and dedicated the next 25 years of his life to teaching philosophy. However, his teachings and the free-thinking nature of philosophers like him posed an existential threat to Emperor Domitian's rule. As a result, Domitian banished all philosophers from the city, leading Epictetus to leave Rome.

Epictetus settled in the newly established city of Nicopolis in ancient Greece. There, he lived a modest and simple life while founding a school of philosophy. For the remainder of his days, he dedicated himself to teaching his philosophical principles until he passed away naturally from old age. His life exemplifies his commitment to Stoic principles despite facing societal constraints and adversity. His teachings continue to resonate with people seeking wisdom and guidance in navigating life's challenges.

At the heart of Epictetus' thoughts and arguments lies a fundamental teaching centered on the concept of control. The dichotomy of control emphasizes the difference between what is within our control and what is not (Vecchiola, 2022b). The path to happiness, also called eudaimonia, is found by correctly identifying what is in our control and focusing our efforts on those things.

Epictetus on Control

In his *Enchiridion*, Epictetus wrote:

> "Some things are within our power, while others are not. Within our power are opinion, motivation, desire, aversion, and, in a word, whatever is of our own doing; not within our power are our body, our property, reputation,

office, and, in a word, whatever is not of our own doing." (Weaver, 2019b)

In the realm of addiction, individuals often struggle with the aspects of their lives that lie beyond their control. Their body, cravings, and physical dependence on substances are examples of external factors that they cannot directly govern. Similarly, their reputation, property, and other external circumstances may have been negatively affected by their addiction, but these too are not fully within their control.

However, this quote emphasizes that despite the external challenges posed by addiction, there are crucial aspects within an individual's power. Their opinions, motivations, desires, and aversions are part of what they can control. This speaks to the idea that seeking recovery begins with recognizing and accepting personal responsibility for one's thoughts, choices, and actions.

By acknowledging that certain things are beyond their control, individuals in recovery can focus on those aspects within their power. They can take ownership of their mindset, their willingness to change, and their commitment to sobriety. Through introspection, they can understand their motivations for recovery, recognize triggers and aversions, and cultivate a strong desire for positive change.

Moreover, Epictetus emphasizes the importance of self-compassion in the recovery journey. Recognizing that certain external factors are beyond their control, individuals can learn to be gentle with themselves. Instead of dwelling on past mistakes or events beyond their influence, they can focus on what they can do to improve their lives moving forward.

Embracing the Dichotomy of Control frees us from the burden of trying to control the uncontrollable. It allows us to accept the uncertainty and unpredictability of life and develop the wisdom to discern where to direct our energy and efforts.

While we can strive to influence external circumstances and exert some control over our lives, it takes wisdom to discern which aspects are malleable and which are beyond our reach. Stoicism wants us to focus on what is within our control, such as our thoughts and actions, rather than obsessing over things we cannot change. It encourages us to accept the inevitable defeats and failures that arise when our efforts to shape external events are unsuccessful.

Avoid Becoming Attached to External Things

Given that external circumstances are beyond our control, Stoics caution against developing excessive attachments to them. This encompasses material possessions, societal status, and the opinions of others. Stoic philosophy advises us to cultivate detachment and avoid placing undue importance on these external factors.

Cultivate an Inner Sense of Well-Being

Rather than seeking happiness from external factors, Stoic philosophy highlights the significance of nurturing an internal sense of well-being that remains unaffected by external circumstances. It emphasizes the cultivation of inner strength, resilience, and contentment that are independent of the ups and downs of life. Stoicism encourages individuals to find fulfillment from within themselves, relying on their own virtues, principles, and self-awareness to cultivate lasting happiness.

Practice Resilience and Adaptability

In the face of challenging circumstances beyond our control, Stoic philosophy promotes the skills of resilience and adaptability. It teaches us that we have the power to choose our response to adversity and encourages us to seek meaning and purpose in difficult situations. By adopting a Stoic mindset, we can navigate challenging circumstances with grace and find opportunities for growth and personal development.

Don't Be Afraid of Adversity

Adversity and challenges are inherent aspects of life, and there is no need to fear them. Rather than being apprehensive, Stoicism encourages us to embrace these trials as valuable opportunities for personal growth and self-improvement. With a shift in perspective, we can approach challenges with resilience and a mindset focused on extracting wisdom and strength from each experience.

Embrace the Present Moment

Lastly, the Dichotomy of Control serves as a reminder to embrace the present moment and avoid excessive worry about the future or fixation on the past. When we direct our attention to what is within our control in the present moment, we are aligning our thoughts and actions with nature and reason. This allows us to cultivate a sense of harmony and purpose in our lives. Stoicism asks us to live mindfully and intentionally, making the most of the present while letting go of unnecessary concerns about the future or regrets from the past.

Things Outside Our Control

Here are some aspects of life that Stoicism teaches us are outside of our control.

Death and mortality: Stoics acknowledge that death is an inevitable part of the human experience. While we can take steps to maintain good health and make responsible choices, the timing and circumstances of our mortality are ultimately beyond our control. Stoicism encourages us to accept the finitude of life and live each day with purpose and virtue.

Economic and political conditions: The state of the economy, political climates, and broader societal structures are largely beyond an individual's control. While we can participate in civic engagement and strive for positive change, the ultimate outcome of economic and political events is unpredictable and influenced by numerous factors.

Genetic predispositions and inherited traits: Our genetic makeup and inherited traits, such as physical characteristics and certain predispositions, are aspects of life determined before our birth. Stoics teach us to accept these inherent qualities as part of our individual nature and focus on utilizing our abilities and strengths to the best of our abilities.

Historical events and cultural trends: The course of history and cultural shifts occur on a larger scale and are shaped by countless factors and individuals over time. As individuals, we have limited control over these broader trends. Stoicism encourages us to be mindful of our role within the context of history while focusing on personal growth and contributing positively to our immediate environment.

Natural disasters and weather conditions: Natural disasters and weather patterns are forces of nature that lie beyond human control. Stoicism says to accept these occurrences as part of the natural order and to focus our energy on adapting and responding to them rather than trying to change them.

Other people's thoughts, feelings, and behaviors: We cannot directly control the thoughts, feelings, or behaviors of others. Each individual possesses their own autonomy and agency. Stoicism advocates for focusing on our own actions, thoughts, and emotions, rather than becoming overly concerned with the opinions and actions of others.

The actions of others and their consequences: While we influence and interact with others, their choices and the resulting consequences are ultimately outside of our control. Stoicism asks us to focus on our own actions, leading by example, and responding to the actions of others with wisdom and integrity.

The future and uncertain events: The future is inherently uncertain, and many events are unpredictable or beyond our control. Stoicism emphasizes the importance of embracing the present moment and preparing ourselves to face whatever challenges or opportunities the future may bring.

The opinions and judgments of others: The opinions and judgments that others hold about us are subjective and largely outside of our control. Stoicism dictates not to rely on external validation and instead focus on living according to our own principles and values.

The passage of time and the aging process: The passage of time and the aging process are natural phenomena that occur beyond our control. Stoicism invites us to embrace the present moment and make the most of our time, recognizing that our control lies in how we live our lives.

Things Within Our Control

Here are some things within our control according to Stoicism.

Our actions and behaviors: Stoicism teaches that we have control over our actions and how we choose to behave in different situations. We can make conscious choices to act in accordance with our values and virtues, striving to be morally upright individuals.

Our communication and language use: Stoics believe that we have control over the way we communicate and express ourselves through language. We can choose our words carefully, practicing effective communication and fostering understanding in our interactions with others.

Our emotions and responses to external stimuli: While we may not have direct control over the events and circumstances that trigger our emotions, Stoicism shows us that we can control how we respond to them. We have the power to cultivate emotional intelligence, regulate our emotions, and choose more constructive responses to external stimuli.

Our habits and daily routines: Stoicism emphasizes the importance of developing positive habits and routines that contribute to our well-being. We have control over how we structure our daily lives, incorporating healthy habits and practices that promote personal growth and self-improvement.

Our learning and personal growth: Stoicism encourages lifelong learning and personal growth. We have control over the knowledge we seek, the skills we develop, and the mindset we adopt. By actively pursuing growth and expanding our understanding of the world, we can continually evolve and improve as individuals.

Our personal values and beliefs: Our personal values and beliefs are within our control. Stoicism wants us to reflect on our values, examine our beliefs, and align them with virtuous principles. We have the power to shape our worldview and live in accordance with our deeply held convictions.

Our physical health and fitness: While some aspects of our physical health may be influenced by external factors, Stoicism maintains that we have control over taking care of our bodies. We can make conscious choices to pursue a healthy lifestyle, including regular exercise, proper nutrition, and self-care practices.

Our social interactions and relationships: Stoicism underscores that we have control over how we engage in social interactions and build relationships. We can choose to cultivate healthy and meaningful connections, practicing empathy, compassion, and understanding in our interactions with others.

Our thoughts and attitudes: Stoicism points out that we have control over our thoughts and attitudes. We can choose to cultivate positive and constructive thinking patterns, challenging negative beliefs and replacing them with more empowering ones. By adopting a Stoic mindset, we can shape our perceptions and interpretations of the world.

Our use of time and how we prioritize our tasks: Stoicism highlights being mindful of how we use our time and how we prioritize our tasks. We have control over how we allocate our time and energy, making conscious choices to focus on what truly matters and aligning our actions with our goals and values.

Stoic Philosophy Applied to Sobriety and Addiction Recovery

A Stoic philosophy applied to sobriety and addiction recovery centrally revolves around the concept of control, as exemplified by Epictetus and others in the Dichotomy of Control. In the context of addiction, the analogy of an *allergy* to substances or behaviors is apt, where individuals recognize their powerlessness once a certain substance enters their system (Vecchiola, 2022b). This admission of powerlessness does not imply complete powerlessness in all aspects of life but acknowledges the limitations in controlling the biochemical processes that unfold in the brain and body upon use.

Stoicism emphasizes moderation, as embodied in the virtue of temperance. While the Stoics might approach substance and non-substance use with caution and rationality given the growing knowledge of its negative health effects, they would also recognize the challenge of remaining sober in a society surrounded by temptations. Stoic teachings encourage individuals to develop a more advanced sense of fitness, enabling them to navigate social pressures and remain sober in the face of external influences.

In addiction recovery, individuals are often advised to avoid triggers related to their addiction initially. However, the Stoics also caution against isolating oneself from society and instead advocate for developing a well-ordered mind that allows individuals to face any situation without relying on substances. A Stoic-based recovery focuses on initiating profound internal changes, cultivating strength of character, and embracing a way of life that enables individuals to navigate life's challenges without resorting to substances.

Living a Stoic way of life in recovery means doing the same activities as others but with a different mindset and approach. It means attending parties, celebrating, mourning, and engaging in relationships without the need for substances. It means developing the resilience to face adversity, the wisdom to learn from mistakes, and the integrity to live according to one's principles and values.

Ultimately, a Stoicism-based recovery empowers individuals to lead fulfilling lives, filled with meaningful connections, personal growth, and a commitment to living in alignment with their values. It provides a roadmap for individuals to navigate the complexities of addiction recovery while cultivating inner strength and serenity.

Stoic Principles for Addiction Recovery

Acknowledge the Lack of Control Over Addiction

Recognizing that addiction is outside of your control is a crucial step in the recovery process. Addiction is a complex condition that involves both physical and psychological factors, and it often develops due to a combination of genetic, environmental, and behavioral influences. Accepting that addiction is beyond your control helps shift the focus from blame and guilt to understanding and seeking appropriate help.

Embrace Discomfort as Part of the Recovery Journey

Embracing discomfort is another essential aspect of addiction recovery. Recovery is a journey that involves facing challenging emotions, triggers, and cravings. It requires stepping out of your comfort zone and confronting the discomfort that arises during the process. Embracing discomfort means being willing to experience temporary discomfort for long-term growth and well-being. It involves acknowledging and sitting with uncomfortable feelings rather than seeking immediate relief through substance use or other addictive behaviors.

Foster Self-Discipline for Personal Growth

Stoicism encourages us to embrace discomfort and challenges as opportunities for growth and learning. Instead of avoiding difficult situations, we can confront them head-on, building resilience and strengthening our resolve to overcome addiction. Developing self-discipline is another key aspect of Stoic philosophy that can greatly aid in recovery. By cultivating self-discipline, we can resist the urges and cravings associated with addictive behaviors, empowering ourselves to make choices aligned with our recovery goals.

Engage in Mindfulness Practices for Increased Awareness

Mindfulness, a practice related to principles espoused by Stoic philosophy, plays a crucial role in addiction recovery. We will explore mindfulness more in Chapter 5. By practicing mindfulness, we can stay present in the moment, observing our thoughts and emotions without judgment. This awareness allows us to recognize and navigate cravings and urges, making conscious choices to avoid relapse.

Direct Your Attention to the Present Moment

Living in the present moment is a central tenet of Stoic philosophy. It teaches us to let go of past regrets and future worries, focusing our attention on the here and now. By directing our energy toward the present, we can maintain a clear mind and avoid being consumed by the weight of addiction.

Discover Meaning and Purpose in Life

Finding meaning and purpose in life is essential for sustaining recovery. Stoicism encourages us to identify our values and align our actions with them. By engaging in activities that give our lives meaning and fulfillment, we can cultivate a sense of purpose that serves as a powerful motivator to stay sober.

Cultivate Resilience to Overcome Challenges

Resilience is a trait emphasized by Stoic philosophy, teaching us to bounce back from setbacks and challenges. In addiction recovery, resilience allows us to persevere through difficult moments and maintain our commitment to sobriety.

Assume Responsibility for Your Choices and Actions

Taking responsibility for our actions is another key principle in Stoicism. By acknowledging our role in addiction and taking ownership of our behaviors, we regain a sense of control and agency over our lives. This self-awareness empowers us to make positive changes and actively participate in our recovery journey.

Nurture a Sense of Gratitude for the Positive Aspects of Life

Cultivating a sense of gratitude is another practice advocated by Stoicism. By focusing on the things we are grateful for, even in the midst of challenges, we can shift our perspective and foster a positive outlook. Gratitude helps us appreciate the progress we have made and find contentment in our recovery journey.

Be Compassionate To Yourself

Lastly, Stoic philosophy reminds us to practice self-compassion. Recovery is not a linear process, and setbacks are to be expected. By showing kindness and understanding towards ourselves, we can navigate the ups and downs of recovery and relapses with resilience and determination.

Conclusion

Embracing the Dichotomy of Control allows individuals to reclaim their agency in addiction recovery and focus their efforts on what truly matters. This is a practical example of how Stoic philosophy provides valuable insights and tools for navigating the complexities of addiction by directing attention to what is within our control and accepting what is outside of it. By recognizing that addiction itself is beyond our control and embracing discomfort as opportunities for growth, you can develop resilience and strengthen resolve to overcome addiction. Cultivating self-discipline, practicing mindfulness, and focusing on the present moment are crucial components of Stoic philosophy that empower individuals to make conscious choices aligned with their recovery goals. Additionally, finding meaning and purpose, practicing resilience, taking responsibility for actions, cultivating gratitude, and practicing self-compassion are essential practices that enable individuals to navigate the ups and downs of recovery with wisdom and strength. By embracing the Dichotomy of Control, individuals embark on a transformative path that leads to lasting sobriety and a life of purpose, resilience, and inner peace.

Chapter 4:

Cultivating Resilience

Through Adversity

In this chapter, we explore how Stoic philosophy can help us cultivate mental and emotional resilience in the face of addiction and life's challenges. Stoicism teaches us to embrace adversity as an opportunity for personal growth and development.

The first section focuses on Stoic principles that contribute to building resilience. We learn to understand and manage difficult emotions, develop self-awareness, and build inner strength. By embracing these principles, we enhance our ability to navigate adversity with composure and resilience.

The second section examines the mindset and attitudes needed to embrace challenges as opportunities. By adopting a growth mindset and specific strategies, we can shift our perspective and see setbacks as stepping stones to growth. This section highlights various approaches and techniques to cultivate resilience and view challenges positively.

Stoicism as a Path to Enhancing Mental Strength and Coping Abilities

Stoicism has long been recognized as a form of resilience training as it aligns with the principles of modern psychology. By integrating cognitive and behavioral skills training, individuals can cultivate resilience and equip themselves to better handle future challenges. In fact, Stoicism and resilience have become closely intertwined, with Epictetus, a prominent Stoic teacher, being referred to as the "patron saint of the resilient" by contemporary expert Michael Neenan (Robertson, 2020).

The foundational concepts of cognitive-behavioral therapy draw inspiration from Stoic philosophy, particularly the *cognitive theory of emotion*. This theory posits that our emotions are significantly influenced by our underlying beliefs or cognitions. Building upon this philosophical heritage, Stoic Mindfulness and Resilience Training (SMRT) was developed as an intensive four-week program, delivered in an e-learning format.

Since its inception in 2014, SMRT has attracted over 500 participants, showcasing remarkable outcomes. According to Robertson (2020), pre- and post-training measures have demonstrated significant improvements in various areas:

- Satisfaction with life increased by 27%

- Positive emotions increased by 16%

- Reduction in negative emotions by 23%

- Flourishing experienced a boost of 17%

These findings highlight the efficacy of Stoic principles and practices in fostering resilience, enhancing well-being, and promoting personal growth.

Marcus Aurelius on Obstacles

In his *Meditations*, Marcus Aurelius penned a saying that, rephrased, has become a famous Stoic quote: "The impediment to action advances action. What stands in the way becomes the way" (Cloos, 2019). This passage encourages the reader to view obstacles and challenges as opportunities for growth and progress. Just like a hiker who uses a rock on the path to step higher and overcome the obstacle, we can use setbacks as stepping stones toward achieving our goals.

While this isn't written as a parable, it can be interpreted as such. Here's what Aurelius writes in *Meditations*, 5.20:

> "…so far as some men make themselves obstacles to my proper acts, man becomes to me one of the things which are indifferent, no less than the sun or wind or a wild beast. Now it is true that these may impede my action, but they are no impediments to my affects and disposition, which have the power of acting conditionally and changing: for the mind converts and changes every hindrance to its

activity into an aid; and so that which is a hindrance is made a furtherance to an act; and that which is an obstacle on the road helps us on this road." (2017b)

When applied to addiction and recovery, this quote from Marcus Aurelius holds profound insights. In the context of addiction, "some men" could refer to the influence of external factors or even individuals who may tempt, enable, or discourage someone from pursuing their path to recovery. These external influences can be likened to the sun, wind, or a wild beast, as they may obstruct the journey towards healing and sobriety.

However, Marcus Aurelius points out that while these external influences may hinder one's physical actions or access to substances, they do not have the power to control one's inner emotions and attitudes. The addict's affects and disposition, though challenged by external circumstances, have the potential to act conditionally and change. This suggests that despite the obstacles posed by external factors, individuals in recovery still have agency over their thoughts, emotions, and choices.

The mind, as Marcus Aurelius describes, has the remarkable ability to transform hindrances into aids. This means that even when faced with difficult situations or temptations, those in recovery can use these challenges as opportunities for growth and progress. Rather than viewing external obstacles as roadblocks, they can choose to see them as stepping stones on the path to recovery.

In essence, this quote reminds those in recovery that while external influences may present challenges, they should not be perceived as insurmountable barriers. By cultivating a resilient and determined mindset, individuals can transform obstacles into opportunities for personal growth and reinforce their commitment to sobriety. The journey to recovery may have its difficulties, but the power lies within each person to navigate those challenges, overcome hindrances, and continue progressing towards a healthier and fulfilling life.

Nurturing Inner Strength and Endurance Amidst Challenges

The Stoic philosophy enlightens us that individuals who flourish in the midst of adversity don't rely solely on positive thinking. Instead, they adopt a transformative perspective that allows for an objective understanding of their circumstances (McLane, 2020). By directing their attention to what is within their control, they actively work towards improving unfavorable situations. Moreover, they embrace the expectation of encountering challenges and, above all, demonstrate unwavering perseverance.

Resilience is the capacity to recover and adapt when confronted with demanding life circumstances, enabling us to withstand and manage them without being consumed by overwhelming emotions (Robertson,

2022). Emotional resilience equips individuals with the ability to effectively cope with a wide range of challenging situations. These may include significant setbacks like financial hardship, academic or career setbacks, relationship difficulties, health issues, the ending of important relationships, or the experience of personal trauma.

In the face of life's challenges, it is necessary to cultivate resilience in order to navigate adversity and emerge stronger. Stoic principles provide valuable guidance for building mental and emotional resilience, offering a practical framework to confront difficulties with strength, adaptability, and a positive mindset. By incorporating these principles into our lives, we can develop inner fortitude, maintain emotional balance, and discover meaning even amidst adversity.

By adopting the perspective that challenges are not insurmountable obstacles, but rather opportunities for growth, we undergo a transformative shift in our mindset. This change allows us to approach difficulties with determination and a sense of possibility. Embracing challenges as opportunities enables us to cultivate resilience by developing the necessary skills, knowledge, and inner strength to overcome them. It empowers us to see setbacks as stepping stones toward personal growth and self-improvement.

In the realm of cultivating resilience through adversity, a deciding aspect lies in developing mental performance. Mental performance revolves around being prepared, maintaining focus on the present moment, and making informed predictions about the future (Haselhuhn, 2018). We can utilize mental cues to remain engaged in the present, and strive to anticipate the outcomes of our potential actions based on the current circumstances.

Stoic Principles to Build Mental and Emotional Resilience

Incorporating these principles into our lives helps us build mental and emotional resilience. By developing inner strength, maintaining emotional balance, and cultivating a resilient mindset, we can navigate life's challenges with greater equanimity and adaptability. These principles provide a practical framework for finding meaning, maintaining motivation, and fostering personal growth even in the face of adversity.

Accepting Difficult Emotions as a Natural Part of Life

Accepting difficult emotions as a natural part of life is a foundational principle in building mental and emotional resilience. Stoicism teaches us that it is normal to experience a wide range of emotions, including sadness, anger, fear, and frustration. By acknowledging and accepting these emotions, we avoid suppressing or denying them, allowing us to process and navigate them in a healthy way. This acceptance enables us to develop emotional resilience and a greater understanding of ourselves.

Building Emotional Intelligence and Self-Awareness

Building emotional intelligence and self-awareness is essential in cultivating resilience. Emotional intelligence involves recognizing and understanding our own emotions as well as those of others and effectively managing them. By developing emotional intelligence, we enhance our ability to navigate challenging situations with empathy, compassion, and self-control. Self-awareness, on the other hand, involves having a deep understanding of our thoughts, feelings, strengths, and limitations. It allows us to identify our triggers and patterns of behavior, empowering us to respond more skillfully to adversity and build resilience.

Building Resilience Through Exposure to Challenges and Obstacles

Resilience is not developed in a vacuum; it requires exposure to challenges and obstacles. Stoicism teaches us that we must actively seek out and engage with difficult experiences to build resilience. Each challenge we face presents an opportunity for growth and learning. By intentionally stepping out of our comfort zones, we develop problem-solving skills, adaptability, and discover our inner strength. Stoicism encourages us to embrace challenges as necessary components of our personal development and to actively engage with them to build resilience.

Cultivating a Sense of Detachment from External Circumstances

Cultivating a sense of detachment from external circumstances is a key principle in Stoicism and resilience-building. It involves recognizing that we cannot control everything that happens around us. Instead of becoming overly attached to outcomes or external events, Stoicism teaches us to focus on what is within our control—our thoughts, actions, and attitudes. By letting go of the need to control external factors, we reduce stress and anxiety, enabling us to approach challenges with greater clarity and composure.

Cultivating a Sense of Purpose and Direction

Having a sense of purpose and direction is a powerful tool in building resilience. Stoicism emphasizes the importance of reflecting on our values, passions, and what truly matters to us. By cultivating a sense of purpose, we have a guiding compass that helps us navigate challenges and setbacks with determination and resilience. It provides us with the motivation and inner strength necessary to persevere in the face of adversity.

Cultivating Gratitude and a Positive Outlook

Cultivating gratitude and maintaining a positive outlook are instrumental in building resilience. Stoicism encourages us to practice gratitude by consciously acknowledging and appreciating the positive aspects of our lives, even in the midst of challenges. By focusing on what we are grateful for, we shift our perspective and foster a resilient and optimistic mindset. This positive outlook helps us find strength, hope, and meaning during difficult times, enabling us to bounce back and persevere.

Developing a Growth Mindset and Viewing Challenges as Opportunities

Developing a growth mindset is a fundamental Stoic principle in resilience-building. It involves viewing challenges as opportunities for personal growth and learning. Rather than perceiving setbacks as failures, a growth mindset allows us to see them as valuable lessons and stepping stones on our journey. This perspective empowers us to approach challenges with curiosity, adaptability, and a belief in our ability to learn and improve. By developing a growth mindset, we transform obstacles into opportunities for resilience and personal development.

Developing Coping Mechanisms for Stress and Anxiety

To build mental and emotional resilience, it is crucial to develop healthy coping mechanisms for stress and anxiety. Stoicism offers various techniques and practices to manage these challenges. This may include mindfulness exercises, deep breathing techniques, physical activity, journaling, or seeking support from trusted individuals. By cultivating effective coping strategies, we enhance our ability to manage stress, reduce anxiety, and bounce back from adversity more effectively.

Embracing Adversity as an Opportunity for Growth

Stoicism encourages us to embrace adversity as an opportunity for growth and personal development. Rather than fearing or avoiding difficult situations, Stoic philosophy teaches us to face them head-on. By reframing adversity as a pathway to growth, we approach it with courage, determination, and an unwavering belief in our ability to overcome challenges. Embracing adversity allows us to develop resilience, learn valuable lessons, and discover our inner strength.

Emphasizing the Importance of Personal Responsibility

Personal responsibility is a core principle in Stoicism and resilience-building. It involves taking ownership of our thoughts, actions, and choices. By recognizing that we have agency over our lives and the ability to shape our responses to challenges, we regain a sense of control. Emphasizing personal responsibility allows us to proactively address obstacles, learn from our mistakes, and actively participate in our own growth and resilience-building journey.

Focusing on the Present Moment and Avoiding Dwelling on the Past or Future

Focusing on the present moment is essential in building resilience. Stoicism emphasizes the importance of directing our attention and efforts to what is within our control in the here and now. By grounding ourselves in the present, we cultivate mindfulness and develop a clear and focused mindset. This focus enables us to effectively respond to challenges, make proactive choices, and maintain resilience in the face of adversity.

Focusing on What Is Within Our Control

Stoicism teaches us to focus on what is within our control, rather than becoming consumed by external circumstances. While we cannot control the actions of others or the outcomes of certain events, we have agency over our thoughts, attitudes, and behaviors. By directing our energy toward what we can control, we develop a sense of empowerment and resilience. This focus enables us to make proactive choices, adapt to challenges, and maintain inner strength in the face of adversity.

Learning to Manage Negative Self-Talk and Limiting Beliefs

Learning to manage negative self-talk and limiting beliefs is crucial for building resilience. Stoicism emphasizes the power of our thoughts and the importance of challenging negative narratives. By cultivating self-compassion, practicing positive affirmations, and challenging self-limiting beliefs, we can replace negative self-talk with more empowering and resilient thoughts. This shift in mindset enhances our ability to navigate challenges and setbacks with resilience and a positive outlook.

Practicing Self-Discipline and Self-Control

Practicing self-discipline and self-control is a cornerstone of Stoicism and resilience-building. It involves developing the ability to regulate our thoughts, emotions, and behaviors. By exercising self-discipline, we can make conscious choices aligned with our values and goals, even in the face of challenges or temptations. Self-control allows us to resist impulsive reactions, maintain focus, and persevere in the pursuit of our resilience-building objectives.

Practicing Self-Reflection and Introspection

Practicing self-reflection and introspection is a powerful tool for building resilience. Taking time to reflect on our experiences, emotions, and responses helps us gain insight into our strengths, weaknesses, and areas for growth. By engaging in introspection, we enhance self-awareness, identify patterns, and develop strategies for personal development. Self-reflection allows us to make adjustments, learn from our experiences, and continuously grow in resilience.

Embracing Challenges as Opportunities

You can proactively embrace challenges you will encounter as opportunities for personal growth and resilience. These strategies empower individuals to approach difficulties with determination, adaptability, and a positive mindset, ultimately transforming challenges into catalysts for personal development.

Adopting a Growth Mindset

Embracing challenges as opportunities requires adopting a growth mindset. A growth mindset is a belief that our abilities and intelligence can be developed through dedication, effort, and learning from experiences. By embracing a growth mindset, we view challenges as a chance to learn, improve, and expand our capabilities. This mindset shift allows us to approach difficulties with enthusiasm and curiosity, enabling us to persevere and grow in the face of adversity.

Being Patient

Patience is a vital quality when it comes to embracing challenges as opportunities. It is essential to understand that personal growth and overcoming obstacles take time. Patience allows us to navigate challenges without becoming discouraged or giving up prematurely. By cultivating patience, we develop the resilience to persist through setbacks and setbacks, ultimately reaching our goals.

Believing in Yourself

Belief in oneself is a powerful motivator when facing challenges. It involves having confidence in your abilities, strengths, and capacity to overcome obstacles. By believing in yourself, you cultivate a positive self-image and the determination to face challenges head-on. This self-belief serves as a source of inspiration and resilience during difficult times.

Celebrating Small Wins

Acknowledging and celebrating small wins is crucial in building resilience. When facing challenges, it's important to recognize and appreciate the progress made along the way. By celebrating small victories, we maintain motivation, boost self-confidence, and reinforce a positive mindset. These incremental successes serve as stepping stones toward larger goals, fostering resilience and perseverance.

Developing a Plan

Developing a well-thought-out plan is central to effectively embracing challenges. A clear plan helps us navigate obstacles with purpose and direction. It outlines the necessary steps, identifies potential roadblocks, and provides a framework for success. By having a plan in place, we feel more prepared and empowered to tackle challenges, fostering resilience and adaptability.

Embracing Change

Challenges often come with change, and embracing change is a key to growth and resilience. Rather than resisting or fearing change, we assume it as an opportunity for learning and personal development. Embracing change allows us to adapt, acquire new skills, and expand our perspectives. By viewing change as a positive catalyst for growth, we develop the resilience to navigate transitions and thrive in the face of uncertainty.

Embracing Discomfort

Growth and resilience require stepping out of our comfort zones and embracing discomfort (Ye, 2019). By willingly facing uncomfortable situations, we challenge ourselves to grow and expand our capabilities. Embracing discomfort builds resilience by increasing our tolerance for adversity, enhancing problem-solving skills, and fostering adaptability. It enables us to face challenges head-on and discover our true potential.

Focusing on What You Can Control

When embracing challenges, it's important to focus on what is within our control. We have learned through the Dichotomy of Control that we cannot control external circumstances or outcomes, but we can control our responses, attitudes, and actions. By directing our energy toward what we can control, we maintain a sense of empowerment and resilience. This focus enables us to make proactive choices, adapt to challenges, and preserve our inner strength.

Keeping a Positive Attitude

A positive attitude is a powerful asset when facing challenges as opportunities. It involves maintaining an optimistic and hopeful outlook, even in the face of difficulties. By cultivating a positive attitude, we shift our perspective and approach challenges with resilience and determination. Positivity enables us to stay motivated, find solutions, and bounce back from setbacks.

Learning from Failure

Failure is an integral part of the learning process and an opportunity for growth. Embracing challenges involves seeing failure as a valuable lesson rather than a reflection of personal worth. By learning from failure, we gain insights, adjust our strategies, and improve our skills. Viewing failure as a stepping stone toward success enhances resilience, perseverance, and continuous improvement.

Practicing Resilience and Self-Awareness

Actively practicing resilience and self-awareness strengthens our ability to embrace challenges as opportunities. Resilience involves bouncing back from setbacks, adapting to change, and persisting in the face of adversity. Self-awareness allows us to understand our strengths, limitations, and emotional responses, empowering us to navigate challenges effectively. By practicing resilience and self-awareness, we cultivate the inner strength needed to embrace challenges and grow from them.

Reflecting on Your Progress

Regularly reflecting on our progress is crucial for growth and resilience-building. Taking time to evaluate our actions, learn from experiences, and acknowledge our achievements helps us make adjustments and stay on track. Reflection fosters self-awareness, insight, and the ability to refine our strategies. It allows us to celebrate successes, learn from setbacks, and continuously improve our resilience.

Reframing Your Perspective

How we perceive challenges greatly impacts our ability to embrace them as opportunities. Reframing our perspective involves shifting our mindset and looking at challenges from different angles. By reframing challenges as opportunities to learn, grow, and develop new skills, we transform them into catalysts for resilience. This shift in perspective enables us to approach challenges with optimism and resourcefulness.

Seeing Challenges as Opportunities to Learn and Grow

Viewing challenges as opportunities for learning and personal growth is essential. Instead of seeing them as obstacles or threats, we recognize that challenges provide valuable experiences and lessons. Embracing challenges as opportunities allows us to develop new skills, gain insights, and expand our capabilities. This mindset shift fosters resilience, curiosity, and a continuous drive for improvement.

Seeking Out Support

Embracing challenges becomes easier when we seek support from others. Surrounding ourselves with a network of trusted individuals provides encouragement, guidance, and different perspectives. Supportive relationships and communities offer a sense of belonging and the reassurance that we are not alone in our journey. Seeking out support builds resilience by offering emotional support, practical advice, and shared experiences.

Setting Achievable Goals

Setting achievable goals is crucial for embracing challenges effectively. Goals provide direction, focus, and a sense of purpose. By setting realistic and attainable goals, we can break down challenges into manageable steps, fostering resilience and motivation. Achieving these smaller milestones along the way reinforces our belief in our abilities and fuels our progress.

Staying Motivated and Open to Learning

Maintaining motivation and being open to learning are key factors in embracing challenges as opportunities. Motivation propels us forward, even when faced with obstacles. It keeps us committed and determined to overcome challenges. Additionally, staying open to learning allows us to acquire new knowledge, skills, and perspectives. It enables us to adapt to changing circumstances, expand our horizons, and continuously grow in resilience.

Staying Optimistic

Optimism plays a significant role in embracing challenges as opportunities. It involves maintaining a positive outlook and believing in the possibility of positive outcomes. Optimism fuels resilience by providing hope, strength, and a constructive mindset. By staying optimistic, we approach challenges with confidence, perseverance, and the belief that we can overcome them.

Conclusion

By adopting Stoic principles and practices, we can embrace challenges as opportunities for growth and cultivate resilience. Stoicism aligns with modern psychological theories, such as cognitive behavioral therapy (CBT), and has been proven effective in improving well-being. Nurturing strength and endurance, practicing self-reflection, reframing perspectives, and seeking support enhance our ability to navigate hardships and develop resilience. By integrating these principles into our lives, we transform adversity into opportunities for growth and discover our inner strength. Cultivating resilience involves acknowledging difficult emotions, building emotional intelligence, and developing coping mechanisms. It also includes gratitude, maintaining optimism, and setting achievable goals. Celebrating small victories and seeking support from others play essential roles in maintaining motivation and a sense of belonging on our resilience journey.

Chapter 5:

Practicing Mindfulness and

Self-Awareness

In today's demanding world, cultivating resilience is crucial. This chapter explores how integrating Stoic philosophy with mindfulness and self-awareness enhances our ability to respond to challenges. By identifying triggers, cultivating self-awareness, and practicing mindfulness, we can grow personally and develop resilience.

The Roman Stoics linked the goals of achieving tranquility and virtue, often discussing both concepts together. They emphasized that virtue leads to tranquility as a significant benefit. Epictetus, in his Discourses, advises pursuing virtue while highlighting its promise to bring happiness, calmness, and serenity (Irvine, 2009). In fact, he identifies serenity as the ultimate goal that virtue aims to achieve. When someone lacks tranquility, being distracted by negative emotions like anger or grief, they may struggle to act in accordance with their reason. Emotions can overpower their intellect, leading to confusion about what truly matters and hindering their pursuit of virtuous actions.

As a consequence, they might fail to recognize and achieve genuine goodness in their life.

We highlight trigger responses and practical steps for self-awareness. By reflecting, observing thoughts and emotions, and seeking feedback, we gain understanding and make conscious choices. Mindfulness techniques like breath focus and gratitude deepen awareness and reduce stress.

Mindfulness also helps address addiction triggers. It heightens awareness of cravings and emotions, enabling conscious choices and healthier coping mechanisms. By integrating Stoic principles with mindfulness and self-awareness, individuals embark on a transformative journey of recovery and personal growth.

Trigger Responses

Trigger responses are instinctive reactions that individuals may experience when faced with challenging situations or stressors. When an individual experiences a trigger, it signifies that they are encountering a powerful and uncomfortable emotional response to a stimulus that would not typically evoke such a reaction (Cooks-Campbell, 2022). These responses can significantly influence how we perceive and handle adversity. Understanding these trigger responses is crucial as it allows us to gain insight into our automatic reactions and empowers us to develop healthier coping strategies. Let's explore each trigger response in more detail.

Fight

This response involves a tendency towards aggression and confrontation. When confronted with a difficult situation, some individuals may feel compelled to engage in conflict, either verbally or physically. This response often arises from a desire to protect oneself or assert control over the situation. While assertiveness can be beneficial in certain circumstances, unchecked aggression can lead to further complications and hinder effective problem-solving.

Flight

Flight is characterized by an inclination to avoid or escape from the situation. When faced with challenges, individuals who exhibit this response may feel an overwhelming urge to withdraw or flee. This response often stems from a sense of fear or discomfort. While fleeing may provide temporary relief, it can limit personal growth and hinder the development of effective coping mechanisms.

Freeze

The freeze response involves feeling stuck or unable to take action when confronted with adversity. Individuals experiencing this response may feel paralyzed or overwhelmed, making it challenging to respond or make decisions. This reaction often arises from a sense of helplessness or a perceived lack of control.

Recognizing and addressing this response is crucial for breaking through inertia and finding constructive ways to navigate challenges.

Fawn

Fawning is a response characterized by attempting to please others to avoid conflict or maintain harmony. Individuals exhibiting this response may excessively prioritize the needs and desires of others, neglecting their own well-being. Fawning can stem from a fear of rejection or a desire to avoid confrontation. However, over time, this response may lead to resentment, emotional exhaustion, and an erosion of personal boundaries.

Denial

Denial involves refusing to acknowledge or accept the reality of a situation. When faced with adversity, individuals may engage in denial as a defense mechanism to protect themselves from emotional pain or discomfort. However, denying the existence or impact of challenges can prevent individuals from addressing and effectively coping with them, ultimately impeding personal growth and resilience.

Rationalization

Rationalization is a response that involves making excuses or justifications for a situation. Individuals may engage in rationalization to alleviate feelings of guilt, shame, or responsibility. While rationalization can provide temporary relief, it can hinder personal growth by perpetuating patterns of behavior that may not be aligned with our values or well-being.

Projection

Projection is a response where individuals attribute their own thoughts, feelings, or behaviors to others. It involves shifting blame or responsibility onto external factors rather than taking ownership. This response can limit self-reflection and hinder personal development, as it avoids addressing underlying issues and impedes effective problem-solving.

Minimization

Minimization involves downplaying the severity or impact of a situation. When faced with challenges, individuals may minimize their significance as a way to cope with feelings of overwhelm or inadequacy. However, minimizing challenges can prevent individuals from fully acknowledging and addressing them, inhibiting personal growth and resilience.

Catastrophizing

Catastrophizing is a response characterized by imagining the worst-case scenario in a given situation. Individuals engaging in catastrophizing often exaggerate the potential negative outcomes, intensifying their emotional response and creating unnecessary distress. This response can hinder effective problem-solving and amplify stress levels, making it challenging to approach challenges with clarity and resilience.

Numbing

Numbing involves using substances or engaging in behaviors to avoid or suppress the emotions associated with a situation. Individuals may resort to numbing as a way to temporarily escape or alleviate emotional pain. However, relying on substances or behaviors to numb emotions can hinder personal growth, impede the development of healthy coping mechanisms, and exacerbate the challenges being faced.

Self-Awareness

Self-awareness encompasses the capacity to observe oneself clearly and objectively through contemplation and self-examination. The theory of self-awareness suggests that you are not confined by your thoughts; rather, you actively perceive and ponder your thoughts as a distinct entity (Ackerman, 2020). Developing self-awareness is an essential practice for personal growth, resilience, and overcoming addictions. Self-awareness also plays a crucial role in managing triggers effectively. By developing self-awareness, individuals can recognize their triggers, understand their emotional responses, and gain insight into the underlying causes of their reactions. Through self-reflection and introspection, individuals can explore the patterns, thoughts, and beliefs that contribute to their triggers, allowing them to develop healthier coping mechanisms and responses. Self-awareness empowers individuals to break free from automatic, impulsive reactions and instead respond in a more conscious and intentional manner. By cultivating a deep understanding of our thoughts, emotions, and behaviors, we can align our actions with our values and make conscious choices that lead to lasting change.

Types of Self-Awareness

Public

Public self-awareness refers to being conscious of how one appears to others and often arises in situations where individuals are in the spotlight (Cherry, 2023). This type of self-awareness tends to prompt individuals to conform to social norms and behave in socially acceptable ways. However, it can also lead to evaluation anxiety, causing distress or worry about how others perceive them.

Examples of public self-awareness can be seen when delivering a speech at a conference or performing on stage in front of an audience. In these instances, individuals may be acutely aware of their actions, striving to present themselves in a favorable light and meet the expectations of others.

Private

Private self-awareness, on the other hand, involves individuals becoming aware of specific aspects of themselves in a more personal and private manner (Cherry, 2023). For instance, recognizing one's own reflection in a mirror is an instance of private self-awareness.

Examples of private self-awareness include feeling a surge of excitement in the chest when achieving a personal goal or experiencing a sense of unease in the stomach when facing a difficult decision. These internal experiences are known only to the individual, as they occur within their private self-awareness and are not directly observable by others.

Benefits of Self-Awareness

Practicing self-awareness offers a range of benefits that contribute to personal growth. Firstly, self-awareness allows us to become more proactive in our lives by actively taking control and making intentional choices. It fosters a sense of acceptance, helping us embrace our strengths and weaknesses while striving for self-improvement. This proactive mindset enables us to navigate challenges more effectively and seize opportunities for growth.

Furthermore, self-awareness enables us to see things from the perspective of others. By understanding different viewpoints, we can improve our relationships, enhance empathy, and communicate more effectively

(Ackerman, 2020). It also promotes self-control, enabling us to regulate our emotions and responses in various situations. This self-mastery leads to greater resilience and adaptability.

In addition to interpersonal benefits, self-awareness has a direct impact on our decision-making abilities. When we are aware of our values, goals, and emotions, we can make more informed and aligned choices. By considering the potential outcomes and evaluating our own biases, we improve the quality of our decisions, leading to more favorable results and outcomes.

Steps to Practice Self-Awareness

In the context of Stoicism, self-awareness plays a crucial role in examining our inner world and responding to life's challenges with wisdom and composure. In this section, we will explore practical steps to enhance self-awareness and how they relate to both Stoic philosophy and addiction recovery.

Allocate Daily Time for Self-Reflection

Carving out dedicated time each day for self-reflection creates a space for introspection and deepening self-awareness. Find a quiet and comfortable environment where you can be alone with your thoughts. Use this time to engage in activities such as journaling, meditation, or deep breathing exercises. Through self-reflection, you can gain insights into your thoughts, emotions, and behaviors, helping you navigate the complexities of addiction and cultivate a Stoic mindset.

Be Mindful of Thoughts and Emotions Throughout the Day

Practicing mindfulness throughout the day allows you to observe your thoughts and emotions as they arise. By maintaining present-moment awareness, you can notice the content of your thoughts and the accompanying emotions. This awareness enables you to identify any patterns or triggers that may influence your behavior. Regularly check in with yourself to stay attuned to your inner experiences and deepen your self-awareness.

Cultivate Non-judgment and Self-Compassion

Approaching your thoughts and emotions with a non-judgmental attitude is crucial in developing self-awareness. Rather than labeling your thoughts and emotions as good or bad, simply observe them as they come and go. Embrace self-compassion by treating yourself with kindness, understanding, and forgiveness. Recognize that experiencing a range of emotions is a normal part of being human and use self-compassion to foster a nurturing environment for personal growth.

Explore Your Feelings and Their Underlying Reasons

Taking moments throughout the day to explore your feelings and their underlying reasons can deepen your self-awareness. Ask yourself what you are feeling and why. This simple question opens up a pathway to understanding your emotional landscape and brings awareness to the underlying causes or triggers. Be honest and open with yourself as you delve into the reasons behind your emotions, gaining valuable insights into your inner world.

Tune Into Physical Sensations in Your Body

Your body often provides valuable clues about your emotional state. Pay attention to physical sensations such as tension, tightness, or unease. These sensations serve as signals for underlying emotions or stressors. By tuning into and acknowledging these bodily sensations, you can gain a deeper understanding of your emotional experiences and use this awareness to inform your choices and responses.

Observe How Your Behavior Reflects Your Thoughts and Emotions

Your behavior can serve as a reflection of your thoughts and emotions. Observe how your actions align with your internal experiences. Are there any patterns or discrepancies? Reflect on the ways your behavior may be influenced by your thoughts and emotions. This self-reflection allows you to identify areas for growth, make conscious choices, and align your actions with your values.

Engage in Active Listening During Conversations

Active listening is a valuable skill for self-awareness and effective communication. When engaging in conversations, give your full attention to the speaker. Be present and genuinely interested in understanding their perspective. Avoid interrupting or formulating responses in your mind. By actively listening, you deepen your understanding of others and gain insights into your own communication style and patterns.

Seek Feedback to Gain Insights Into Your Behavior and Communication Style

Feedback from trusted individuals provides valuable insights into your blind spots and areas for improvement. Actively seek feedback from friends, family, or colleagues about your behavior and communication style. Be open to constructive criticism and use it as an opportunity for growth and self-awareness. Feedback allows you to gain a more comprehensive understanding of how your actions impact others and adjust your behavior accordingly.

Reflect on Past Experiences and Lessons Learned

Reflecting on past experiences is an integral part of self-awareness. Consider significant events, successes, failures, and challenges. What lessons did you learn? How have those experiences shaped you? By reflecting on the past, you can identify patterns, strengths, and areas for improvement. This reflection provides valuable insights into your growth journey and helps you make informed choices.

Embrace Mindfulness to Stay Present and Focused

Mindfulness is a powerful practice for staying present, reducing stress, and enhancing self-awareness. Engage in mindfulness techniques such as meditation, breath awareness, or body scans to anchor yourself in the present moment. By focusing on the here and now, you can observe your thoughts, emotions, and sensations without judgment or attachment. Mindfulness deepens your self-awareness and helps you develop a clearer understanding of yourself.

Journal to Reflect on Thoughts and Emotions

Writing in a journal creates a structured and introspective outlet for self-reflection. Set aside regular time to write about your thoughts, emotions, and experiences. Use the journal as a space for self-expression, exploration of your inner world, and gaining clarity. Reflecting on your entries can reveal patterns, growth, and areas where you can make positive changes, further enhancing your self-awareness.

Cultivate Gratitude for Yourself and Others

Cultivating gratitude fosters a positive mindset and deepens self-awareness. Take time each day to appreciate and express gratitude for yourself and others. Acknowledge your strengths, accomplishments, and positive qualities. Recognize the contributions of others and express gratitude towards them. Gratitude shifts your focus towards the positive aspects of your life, cultivating self-awareness and a sense of fulfillment.

Identify and Live By Your Values

Understanding your values is fundamental for self-awareness. Reflect on what truly matters to you and what principles guide your life. Identify your core values and evaluate how they align with your actions and decision-making. By living in alignment with your values, you cultivate a sense of purpose, authenticity, and self-awareness.

Recognize Patterns in Thoughts and Behavior

Patterns often emerge in our thoughts, emotions, and behaviors. Pay attention to recurring thoughts, emotional reactions, or behavioral tendencies. By recognizing these patterns, you gain insights into underlying beliefs, triggers, and areas for growth. This awareness empowers you to make conscious choices and break unhelpful patterns, supporting your journey toward self-awareness and overcoming addictions.

Take Intentional Action Based on Self-Awareness

Self-awareness becomes most valuable when it translates into intentional action. Use the insights gained through self-reflection to make positive changes in your life. Set goals, develop new habits, or adjust your behavior based on your self-awareness. Take ownership of your personal growth journey and make conscious choices aligned with your values and well-being.

Steps to Practice Mindfulness

Mindfulness is the capacity to remain fully present in the current moment and direct our attention to the unfolding experience (Tallon, 2020). It involves consciously redirecting our thoughts away from the past or future and instead immersing ourselves in the present reality. By observing and acknowledging what is happening at the moment, we cultivate a state of heightened awareness and engagement with our immediate surroundings.

The practice of mindfulness aligns closely with Stoic philosophy and also supports individuals in overcoming addiction. By cultivating this skill, individuals can develop a heightened sense of awareness, stay present in the moment, and respond to challenges with wisdom and composure. In the context of addiction recovery, mindfulness plays a vital role in recognizing cravings, managing triggers, and making conscious choices that promote well-being and long-lasting change. Let us explore practical steps to incorporate mindfulness into daily life and enhance the journey of recovery.

Carve Out Daily Mindfulness Time

Allocating dedicated time for mindfulness practice is essential for developing a consistent habit. Set aside a specific time each day to engage in mindfulness exercises, whether it's in the morning, during a lunch break, or before bed. This dedicated time allows you to prioritize self-care and cultivate a deep sense of presence and awareness.

Find a Tranquil Space for Practice

Creating a conducive environment for mindfulness practice enhances the experience and focus. Find a quiet and comfortable space where you can minimize distractions and interruptions. It could be a designated meditation corner, a peaceful room, or even a spot in nature. By selecting a tranquil setting, you can deepen your mindfulness practice and foster a sense of inner calm.

Begin With Breath Awareness

The breath serves as an anchor in mindfulness practice. Begin by directing your attention to the sensation of your breath. Observe the inhalation and exhalation, the rhythm, and the physical sensations associated with breathing. This focus on the breath helps ground you in the present moment and serves as a foundation for further mindfulness exercises.

Observe Thoughts With Detachment

Mindfulness involves observing thoughts without attaching judgment or getting caught up in their content. As you practice mindfulness, thoughts may arise. Rather than getting carried away by them, simply observe them with curiosity and detachment. Recognize that thoughts come and go, and you have the power to choose how to respond to them.

Tune Into Physical Sensations

The body provides valuable cues about your internal state. During mindfulness practice, pay attention to physical sensations such as tension, warmth, or discomfort. Bring awareness to different parts of your body and notice any shifts or changes. This body awareness helps you stay connected to the present moment and deepen your mindfulness practice.

Redirect Focus to the Breath

Inevitably, the mind may wander during mindfulness practice. When you notice your mind drifting away, gently redirect your attention back to your breath (Tallon, 2020). Instead of berating yourself for losing focus, approach it with kindness and understanding. Cultivating this gentle redirection strengthens your ability to stay present and focused.

Cultivate Non-Judgment and Self-Compassion

Non-judgment and self-compassion are fundamental aspects of mindfulness. Embrace a mindset of acceptance and non-judgment toward your thoughts, emotions, and experiences. Treat yourself with kindness, understanding, and self-compassion. By nurturing a compassionate attitude, you create a supportive space for personal growth and self-awareness.

Utilize Guided Meditations and Apps

Guided meditations and mindfulness apps can be valuable tools to support your mindfulness practice. These resources provide structured guidance, soothing voices, and a variety of meditation practices to choose from. Utilize these tools to enhance your focus, deepen your mindfulness experience, and explore different techniques.

Infuse Mindfulness Into Daily Activities

Mindfulness is not limited to formal meditation sessions. Infuse mindfulness into your daily activities, such as eating, walking, or engaging in routine tasks. Bring your full attention to each moment, savoring the experience and engaging all your senses. By incorporating mindfulness into everyday life, you cultivate a continuous state of awareness and presence.

Cultivate Gratitude for the Present Moment

Gratitude is a powerful practice that complements mindfulness. Take moments throughout the day to express gratitude and appreciation for the present moment. Notice the beauty in the simple things and reflect on the blessings in your life. Gratitude deepens your mindfulness practice by shifting your focus toward the positive aspects of the present moment (Tallon, 2020).

Embrace Acceptance of What Is

Mindfulness involves accepting reality as it is, without attempting to change or control it. Cultivate an attitude of acceptance and non-resistance towards your thoughts, emotions, and external circumstances. Embrace the present moment without judgment or attachment. This acceptance empowers you to respond skillfully to challenges and find peace amidst uncertainty.

Incorporate Deep Breathing for Relaxation

Deep breathing exercises are an integral part of mindfulness practice. Incorporate deep breaths into your mindfulness routine to induce relaxation and alleviate stress. Focus on slow, intentional inhalations and exhalations, allowing the breath to soothe and ground you in the present moment. Deep breathing enhances your mindfulness practice and promotes overall well-being.

Prioritize Single-Tasking

Mindfulness encourages focusing on one task at a time despite a world filled with distractions. When engaged in an activity, give it your full attention and immerse yourself in the experience. Resist the urge to multitask or be constantly pulled in different directions. By practicing single-pointed focus, you cultivate mindfulness and cultivate a sense of clarity and presence.

Connect Mindfulness with Nature

Connecting with nature enhances mindfulness practice and deepens your sense of interconnectedness. Spend time outdoors, whether it's walking in a park, hiking in the woods, or simply sitting by a river. Observe the natural world around you, engage your senses, and immerse yourself in the present moment. Nature provides a serene backdrop for mindfulness and fosters a deep connection with the Stoic principles of harmony and interconnectedness.

Reflect and Track Progress With Journaling

Journaling is a valuable tool for reflecting on your mindfulness practice and tracking your progress. Set aside time to write about your experiences, insights, and challenges. Reflecting on your journal entries allows you to gain a deeper understanding of your mindfulness journey, identify patterns, and celebrate milestones. Journaling becomes a personal record of your growth and a source of inspiration.

Conclusion

Integrating Stoic philosophy with mindfulness, self-awareness, and self-reflection practices transforms the path to resilience and addiction recovery. By dedicating time to self-reflection and mindfulness, individuals deepen their self-awareness and understanding of inner experiences. Cultivating non-judgment and self-compassion promotes self-acceptance and growth. With self-awareness, individuals align actions with values and navigate addiction with resilience. Mindfulness reduces stress and enhances wise responses to challenges. Integrating Stoic principles with mindfulness and self-awareness fosters recovery, personal growth, and lasting change. These practices help recognize triggers, manage cravings, and make conscious choices. Seeking feedback enhances self-awareness and identifies areas for improvement. Embracing these practices empowers individuals to foster a Stoic mindset and embark on a transformative journey.

Chapter 6:

Cultivating Virtue and

Personal Growth

In this chapter, we explore Stoic virtues and practices relevant to addiction recovery. Wisdom is vital in understanding addiction's root causes and developing coping strategies. Courage encourages individuals to confront challenges and commit to recovery. Temperance fosters self-control, emotional management, and healthy routines. Justice emphasizes making amends, showing compassion, and supporting others in recovery.

We also present Stoic practices for personal growth. Embracing difficulties, finding inspiration, reading and applying knowledge, valuing time, practicing gratitude, acting virtuously, forgiving, finding mental rest, and prioritizing truth are discussed. By integrating these virtues and practices, readers can transform their lives and make significant progress on the path to recovery and self-improvement.

Virtuous Insights: Wisdom From Stoic Philosophers

In the pursuit of addiction recovery, Stoic wisdom can serve as a beacon of guidance and inspiration. Here are some insights offered by Zeno of Citium, Marcus Aurelius, and Epictetus into the essence of virtue and its transformative power. These teachings encourage us to look beyond the fear of consequences or external rewards and embrace the intrinsic value of virtue itself.

Zeno of Citium

"One ought to seek out virtue for its own sake, without being influenced by fear or hope, or by any external influence. Moreover, that in that does happiness consist." (iPerceptive, n.d.)

Zeno's words emphasize the importance of pursuing virtue and sobriety for their inherent value, not just as a means to avoid negative consequences or seek external rewards. Recovery should not be solely driven by fear of the repercussions of addiction or the hope of material gains but by the genuine desire to lead a virtuous and fulfilling life. Happiness in recovery comes from finding purpose and meaning through the practice of virtue itself.

Marcus Aurelius

"What is your art? To be good. And how is this accomplished well except by general principles, some about the nature of the universe, and others about the proper constitution of man?" (iPerceptive, n.d.)

Marcus Aurelius's words highlight the pursuit of being a better person and living virtuously as the ultimate art. To achieve this, individuals in recovery must embrace general principles of Stoicism and self-awareness. Understanding the nature of the universe and recognizing the proper constitution of human behavior can guide them towards making wise decisions and cultivating virtue in their daily lives.

Epictetus

"The soul that companies with Virtue is like an ever-flowing source. It is a pure, clear, and wholesome draught; sweet, rich, and generous of its store; that injures not, neither destroys." (iPerceptive, n.d.)

Epictetus's words offer a beautiful analogy for the soul that aligns itself with virtue. In the context of addiction and recovery, this quote reminds individuals that embracing virtue brings about an inner abundance of peace, clarity, and strength. Virtue acts as a refreshing and replenishing source of well-being, replacing the harmful and destructive nature of addiction. It becomes a constant and unwavering guide on the path to recovery, nurturing the individual with its positive and transformative influence.

Stoic Philosophy Virtues

According to the ancient Stoics, embodying four virtues in our thoughts, beliefs, and actions leads us towards inner tranquility, a fulfilling life, and becoming a constructive contributor to society (Weaver, 2019). They maintained that every situation we encounter, even a challenging or distressing one, presents an opportunity to respond virtuously (Daily Stoic, 2019). By acting in accordance with these virtues, the Stoics believed that other significant aspects of life, such as happiness, success, meaning, reputation, honor, and love, would naturally follow. Let us examine each of the four virtues espoused by the Stoics and apply them to sobriety.

Wisdom

Developing wisdom involves gaining insight into addiction and understanding its root causes and the harm it inflicts. This awareness helps individuals recognize the destructive nature of addictive behaviors and motivates them to seek a different path.

Secondly, wisdom entails the ability to identify triggers that contribute to addictive patterns and the development of effective coping strategies to manage them. By recognizing these triggers and implementing healthy coping mechanisms, individuals can proactively address challenges and avoid relapse.

Self-reflection is an integral component of wisdom. Engaging in introspection allows individuals to examine their thoughts, emotions, and behaviors associated with addiction. By being honest with themselves and cultivating self-awareness, individuals can gain a deeper understanding of their vulnerabilities and strengths, paving the way for personal growth and transformation.

Seeking knowledge and information about addiction and recovery is another facet of wisdom. Actively pursuing education on the subject equips individuals with valuable insights, evidence-based approaches, and a broader perspective on their journey towards recovery.

Lastly, wisdom involves creating a comprehensive recovery plan tailored to individual needs and setting achievable goals. This proactive approach helps individuals structure their path to recovery, maintain focus, and experience a sense of progress and purpose.

Courage

Having the courage to admit that there is a problem and seeking help is a significant step towards recovery. It requires acknowledging vulnerabilities and being open to receiving support and guidance from others. This courageous act sets the foundation for the transformative journey ahead.

Additionally, overcoming fear and anxiety associated with recovery and change is essential. The path to recovery often involves confronting uncomfortable emotions and stepping outside of one's comfort zone. Having the courage to face these fears head-on allows individuals to break free from the constraints of addiction and embrace a new way of life.

Resilience and determination are key attributes of courage in the context of addiction recovery. Facing challenges and setbacks with unwavering resolve and perseverance is crucial for sustained progress. It requires staying focused on the ultimate goal of recovery, even when faced with obstacles along the way.

Taking responsibility for one's actions and making amends is another manifestation of courage in recovery. It involves acknowledging the harm caused by addiction, both to oneself and to others, and being willing to make reparations. By demonstrating accountability, individuals can rebuild trust, foster healing, and move forward in their recovery journey.

Finally, staying committed to the recovery process, even during difficult times, requires immense courage. It entails maintaining motivation, adhering to treatment plans, and actively participating in support systems. This unwavering dedication enables individuals to navigate the ups and downs of recovery and build a solid foundation for long-term sobriety and well-being.

Temperance

One aspect of practicing self-control is avoiding impulsive behavior. It involves pausing and reflecting before acting on immediate desires or cravings. By exercising restraint and considering the potential consequences, individuals can make more mindful and deliberate choices that support their recovery journey.

Regulating emotions and managing stress in healthy ways is another important aspect of self-control. It entails developing strategies and techniques to cope with difficult emotions without turning to addictive substances or behaviors. By practicing emotional resilience and employing healthy coping mechanisms, individuals can navigate challenges and stressors effectively.

Avoiding situations or environments that trigger cravings is a proactive approach to self-control in addiction recovery. It involves identifying triggers and taking necessary steps to minimize exposure to them. By creating a supportive and safe environment, individuals reduce the likelihood of relapse and increase their chances of maintaining sobriety.

Developing a healthy routine and adhering to it is another manifestation of self-control. It involves establishing structured daily habits that promote stability, discipline, and well-being. By incorporating activities such as exercise, meditation, healthy eating, and regular sleep patterns into their routine, individuals cultivate a sense of balance and stability in their lives.

Furthermore, cultivating habits that promote physical and mental well-being is a crucial aspect of self-control in addiction recovery. It entails adopting healthy lifestyle choices, such as engaging in regular exercise, seeking therapy or counseling, practicing mindfulness and relaxation techniques, and surrounding oneself with a supportive network. These habits contribute to overall well-being and support the recovery journey.

Justice

Recognizing the impact of addiction on oneself and others and making amends is an important aspect of growth and healing. It involves acknowledging the consequences of past actions and taking responsibility for them. By making amends, individuals demonstrate humility, integrity, and a commitment to repairing relationships and rebuilding trust.

Treating oneself and others with respect and compassion is a fundamental virtue that fosters empathy and understanding. By practicing self-compassion, individuals cultivate a positive self-image and learn to forgive themselves for past mistakes. Treating others with respect and compassion fosters healthy relationships and a supportive community.

Engaging in community service or other forms of outreach is a way to contribute positively to society and make amends for past actions. By volunteering or helping others in need, individuals not only provide support and assistance but also develop a sense of purpose and fulfillment.

Practicing honesty and integrity in all aspects of life is essential for building trust and maintaining healthy relationships. By being honest with oneself and others, individuals demonstrate authenticity and build a reputation based on integrity. Honesty also involves being accountable for one's actions and maintaining transparency in recovery.

Supporting others in their own recovery journey is a powerful way to give back and contribute to the well-being of others. By offering encouragement, sharing experiences, and providing a listening ear, individuals create a supportive community where everyone can thrive. Supporting others in their recovery also reinforces one's own commitment to personal growth and resilience.

Stoic Practices to Become Your Ideal Self

Stoic philosophy offers guidance on how to cultivate virtues and become your ideal self. Let's explore the following Stoic practices you can implement to promote personal growth and self-improvement in detail:

Embrace Difficulties

The way we respond to life's ups and downs has a profound impact on our destinies. It's not the events themselves that shape us, but rather our reactions to them. Think about the people you admire the most – they have faced immense challenges and emerged stronger. Instead of avoiding difficult situations, see them as opportunities for growth and self-improvement. Every setback, no matter how small, tests us and shapes our character. Remember, everyone faces these tests. By embracing challenges, we cultivate gratitude and learn valuable lessons that enrich our lives.

Find Heroes to Emulate and Who Inspire You

The opening of Marcus Aurelius' *Meditations* teaches us the importance of gratitude for those who shape our character. We learn by observing others, and Marcus expresses gratitude to his grandfather for instilling good morals and self-control, and to his mother for teaching piety and kindness.

In our digital age, we have easy access to the wisdom of great minds. By studying the lives and teachings of virtuous individuals, you gain inspiration and guidance on how to cultivate virtues and live a meaningful life.

Emulating these inspiring individuals allows us to practice what we admire and become positive examples for others. Our efforts to embody their qualities contribute to a world that needs more positive role models.

Read as Often as Possible

Learning to read is the greatest shortcut to understanding and emulating the people we admire.

Access to vast knowledge is at our fingertips, allowing us to tap into the wisdom of centuries. Recognizing our own mortality reinforces the importance of not wasting our limited time on Earth. Countless books offer valuable insights, and it is essential to choose those that are truly useful. Seneca's advice to focus on authors of unquestionable genius remains relevant (Daily Stoic, 2020). Although the pace of life may make reading seem challenging, we have various options to incorporate it into our routines, such as digital books, audiobooks, or articles. By learning from the mistakes and experiences of others, we can save ourselves from repeating them. Even five minutes of reading can make a difference. However, it is crucial to translate the knowledge gained into action. The combination of reading and application is the key to personal growth and self-improvement.

Practice What You Read

The purpose of studying Stoic philosophy is to improve every aspect of our lives. Stoicism is a practical philosophy that helps us overcome destructive emotions and focus on what we can control. It aims to keep us calm under pressure and committed to our ideals. However, reading Stoic texts alone is not enough. We must apply their teachings to our own lives and gain practical experience. By letting go of anger in difficult situations, we discover the peace it brings and become stronger. The books serve as reminders and guidance to prevent us from repeating mistakes and help us navigate challenges with wisdom and resilience.

Stoicism offers practical wisdom for personal growth and a better way of living.

Protect Your Time

One of life's greatest regrets is not staying true to our intentions, leading to wasted time and self-imposed obstacles. By practicing Stoicism, we ensure that we make the most of our allotted time and feel proud of our choices. It's about using each moment to cultivate presence, gratitude, and positive actions, rather than being consumed by negativity and instant gratification (Daily Stoic, 2020). This way, we reach the end of our lives without regrets, having dedicated our time to meaningful work, personal growth, and serving our communities. Embracing what's within our control and fulfilling our responsibilities allows us to be content and grateful for the opportunities we seized.

Appreciate What You Have

Epictetus wisely stated that a wise person does not mourn over what they lack but finds joy in what they have (Ergil, 2021). Similarly, Marcus Aurelius advised us to appreciate the blessings we already possess instead of indulging in fantasies about what we don't have. He urged us to consider how much we would yearn for those blessings if we were without them, encouraging us to cultivate gratitude.

Act Virtuously

We know that the Stoics believed that our ability to become our best selves is directly linked to practicing four key virtues: wisdom, courage, temperance, and justice. Pursuing wisdom helps us learn from every experience, while practicing courage enables us to face challenges without giving up. By cultivating temperance, we avoid emotional excess and maintain self-control. Embodying justice ensures that we consistently strive to do what is morally right. Though not easy, regularly embracing these virtues is the surest path to self-improvement and realizing our ideal selves. Keep these virtues in mind during difficult times and when tested in the coming year, and you will journey toward personal growth and fulfillment.

Practice Forgiveness

Throughout our lives, we inevitably come across individuals who challenge our capacity to forgive. Marcus Aurelius, the Roman Emperor, possessed a deep understanding of this inner conflict. He consciously chose to resist the temptation of seeking revenge, recognizing that it would hinder his personal growth and prevent him from becoming his best self (Daily Stoic, 2020). Marcus understood that holding onto anger and grudges would only diminish his own character. Moreover, he realized that refusing to forgive others, even for minor offenses, would create barriers to self-forgiveness when he made mistakes. Dwelling on past wrongs acts as an obstacle to our progress and development. By embracing forgiveness towards those who have wronged us, we prevent ourselves from carrying the burdensome scars of their actions. Equally important, extending forgiveness to ourselves enables personal growth and the realization of our ideal selves. The act of forgiveness liberates us from the grip of the past, allowing us to move forward and embrace our fullest potential.

Resting the Mind Is Important

In one of his writings, Seneca emphasized the significance of giving the mind proper relaxation, stating that it would rejuvenate and become more focused after a well-deserved break (Ergil, 2021). Although the term *Stoic* has come to represent someone who can endure difficulties without expressing a complaint, it does not imply that they disregarded the importance of rest and relaxation.

Truth Is Your Path

Seneca coined the term euthymia to capture the essence of having peace of mind (Ergil, 2021). According to him, it involves believing in oneself, trusting that we are on the right path, and avoiding doubt by not getting caught up in the multitude of directions others may be heading. Epictetus adds to this by suggesting that we should not demand events to unfold exactly as we wish, but rather embrace them as they naturally occur. By aligning our wishes with reality, we can cultivate a serene and tranquil life.

Conclusion

Stoic philosophy and its application to addiction recovery center around cultivating virtues and personal growth. Wisdom helps understand addiction and develop coping strategies. Courage empowers individuals to face challenges and commit to recovery. Temperance fosters self-control and healthy routines. Justice guides making amends and supporting others. Stoic practices, such as embracing difficulties, seeking inspiration, valuing time, practicing gratitude, and aligning with truth, aid personal growth. Integrating these virtues and practices brings transformation, resilience, and progress in recovery. By embodying Stoic principles, individuals navigate addiction, find purpose, and foster lasting recovery and self-improvement.

Chapter 7:

Seeking Wisdom Through

Reflection and Learning

The Stoics believed in continuous personal growth and self-improvement through reflection and self-criticism. They constantly evaluated their actions and sought areas for enhancement. In the context of sobriety, reflecting on past experiences is transformative, providing valuable insights and lessons. Self-reflection and learning enable alternative approaches and informed decisions. Keeping a journal, seeking support, practicing self-compassion, setting realistic goals, and embracing Stoic practices foster clarity, resilience, and personal growth in recovery.

Epictetus outlines several signs of progress in our Stoic journey (Irvine, 2009). As we advance, we'll stop blaming, criticizing, and praising others. Our tendency to boast about our knowledge will diminish. Instead of faulting external circumstances when our desires are unmet, we'll take responsibility for our reactions. Gaining mastery over our desires will lead to fewer of them; our impulses toward various things will decrease. Most significantly, we'll no longer view ourselves as a friend who must fulfill every desire but rather as an enemy lying in wait, recognizing the need to restrain and discipline ourselves.

Stoic Teachings to Understand Oneself and Addiction

According to Stoic philosophy, the experience of pain should be approached with the same endurance and acceptance as pleasure. For example, the use of drugs such as marijuana can provide an escape from facing and addressing problems directly by altering one's state of consciousness (Quantumplatonics, 2015). Excessive consumption of alcohol is also considered a vice, as expressed by the philosopher Seneca who stated that vices carry their own consequences (Tosin, 2023b). Excessive drinking can lead to various physical health issues, including liver disease, heart disease, and different forms of cancer. These consequences serve as a form of *punishment* resulting from indulging in such vices. Here are additional Stoic teachings that can be applied to enhance self-awareness and gain a deeper understanding of oneself and one's addiction.

Reflecting on Personal History and Past Traumas

Reflecting on personal history and past traumas or experiences is an important first step. Stoicism encourages introspection and self-examination to uncover any underlying factors that may have contributed to addiction. By examining these aspects, individuals can gain insights into the root causes and work towards addressing them effectively.

Identifying Triggers and High-Risk Situations

Identifying triggers and high-risk situations is crucial in developing strategies to avoid relapse. Stoic teachings emphasize the need to be aware of external factors that can lead to substance use or addictive behavior. By identifying these triggers, individuals can proactively plan alternative responses and develop healthier coping mechanisms.

Keeping a Journal for Thought and Behavior Tracking

Keeping a journal serves as a valuable tool for tracking thoughts, emotions, and behaviors related to addiction. Stoicism promotes self-reflection, and journaling provides a means to gain clarity and self-awareness. By regularly recording experiences, individuals can identify patterns, triggers, and progress, fostering personal growth and recovery.

Seeking Support From Therapists, Counselors, or Support Groups

Seeking support from therapists, counselors, or support groups aligns with Stoic principles of recognizing the value of community and seeking guidance. Engaging in therapy or participating in support groups offers a safe space to share experiences, gain insights, and learn from others facing similar challenges. These connections can provide encouragement, accountability, and a sense of belonging.

Practicing Self-Compassion and Avoiding Self-Blame

Practicing self-compassion is essential in the recovery journey. Stoicism emphasizes the importance of treating oneself with kindness and understanding. By cultivating self-compassion, individuals can let go of self-blame or shame, fostering a more positive mindset and allowing for healing and growth.

Understanding the Science of Addiction

Learning about the science behind addiction and its effects on the brain and behavior provides a rational understanding of the condition. Stoic teachings value knowledge and understanding as a means to make informed choices. By learning about the science of addiction, individuals can develop a deeper comprehension of its mechanisms, which can aid in developing effective coping strategies and approaches to recovery.

Challenging Negative Beliefs About Addiction and Recovery

Identifying and challenging negative or distorted beliefs about addiction and recovery is crucial for personal growth. Stoicism encourages critical thinking and examining one's beliefs. By questioning and challenging negative beliefs, individuals can reshape their perspectives and adopt a more positive and empowering mindset, supporting their journey towards recovery.

Recognizing the Impact on Relationships, Career, and Well-Being

Recognizing the impact of addiction on relationships, careers, and overall well-being is an important aspect of self-awareness. Stoic teachings encourage individuals to acknowledge the consequences of their actions. By recognizing the broader impact of addiction, individuals can cultivate motivation for change and make amends where necessary.

Setting Realistic Goals and Tracking Progress

Setting realistic goals for recovery and tracking progress aligns with Stoic principles of personal growth and continuous improvement. By setting achievable goals, individuals create a sense of direction and purpose. Regularly monitoring progress provides a tangible measure of success and reinforces commitment to the recovery journey.

Taking Responsibility and Making Amends

Taking responsibility for one's actions and making amends when necessary is essential for personal growth and healing. Stoicism emphasizes the virtue of integrity and accountability. By taking ownership of past actions, individuals can work towards making amends, rebuilding trust, and fostering positive change in their lives and relationships.

Practicing Mindfulness and Self-Awareness

Practicing mindfulness and self-awareness helps individuals identify patterns of thought and behavior. Stoic teachings highlight the importance of being present in the moment and observing one's thoughts and actions. By cultivating mindfulness, individuals can develop a heightened awareness of their triggers, cravings, and emotional states, enabling them to respond in a more intentional and constructive manner.

Learning Coping Strategies for Cravings and Symptoms

Learning coping strategies to manage cravings and addiction-related symptoms is an integral part of the recovery process. Stoicism promotes the development of practical tools for navigating challenges. By learning and implementing effective coping strategies, individuals can effectively manage cravings and develop healthier alternatives to addictive behaviors.

Building a Supportive Network

Building a supportive network of friends and family who understand and support the recovery journey is essential. Stoic teachings emphasize the value of surrounding oneself with virtuous individuals. By fostering meaningful connections with supportive individuals, individuals create a positive environment that promotes growth, accountability, and encouragement.

Prioritizing Self-Care for Physical and Mental Health

Practicing self-care and prioritizing physical and mental health is crucial for overall well-being. Stoicism recognizes the importance of taking care of oneself to navigate life's challenges effectively. By prioritizing self-care, individuals can address their physical and mental health needs, enhancing their resilience and supporting their recovery journey.

Maintaining Commitment to Daily Recovery

Maintaining a commitment to recovery and making it a daily priority is central to Stoic philosophy. Stoicism emphasizes the importance of consistency and discipline in pursuing personal growth. By making recovery a daily priority, individuals reinforce their commitment, cultivate resilience, and ensure ongoing progress on their journey toward lasting sobriety and self-improvement.

Stoic Practices for Recovery

Here are some Stoic practices encompassing a range of techniques that help individuals develop, reflect and learn, allowing them to effectively navigate challenges, regulate their emotions, and cultivate a profound sense of inner peace. By integrating these Stoic practices into their journey of recovery, individuals can elevate their emotional sobriety, nurture resilience, and foster a greater sense of self-awareness and acceptance.

Journaling

The Stoic philosophers, despite their diverse backgrounds and life experiences, shared a common practice that contributed to their enduring legacy: journaling. Whether as an emperor like Marcus Aurelius, a slave like Epictetus, or a power-broker and playwright like Seneca, they all devoted time to documenting their inner thoughts (Avalon Malibu, 2020). In the realm of recovery, writing or journaling is often encouraged as a valuable tool for self-discovery. Through writing, we gain a deeper understanding of ourselves. Marcus Aurelius, for instance, found solace in journaling at the end of each day, recognizing the therapeutic effect it had on his sleep. Journaling provides a constructive outlet for processing negative emotions and relieving stress. It allows us to reflect, release, and transform our inner struggles into personal growth.

Through journaling, individuals can embark on a journey of self-reflection and self-improvement. By delving into their experiences, they gain deeper insights into their triggers, challenges, and victories. They can explore the underlying patterns of thought and behavior that may hinder their recovery progress. Recognizing these patterns allows individuals to become more aware of their thought processes and make conscious choices that align with their recovery goals.

Gratitude becomes a focal point in the journaling practice. Individuals are encouraged to shift their attention to the positive aspects of their lives, cultivating an attitude of appreciation. By actively noting and acknowledging the things they are grateful for, individuals develop a more optimistic outlook and strengthen their resilience. This practice aligns with the

Stoic principle of focusing on what is within one's control and finding contentment in the present moment.

In the context of addiction recovery, journaling serves as a tool for reinforcing one's commitment to recovery. By documenting their progress, challenges, and insights, individuals can review and reflect on their journey. Journaling becomes a tangible reminder of their dedication to change and provides a source of motivation during difficult times. It helps individuals stay accountable to themselves and their recovery goals.

Training Perceptions

According to Stoic philosophy, there is no inherent good or bad in events themselves; it is our perceptions that assign value to them (Avalon Malibu, 2020). This perspective highlights that every occurrence is objective, and it is our interpretation that labels it as either positive or negative. The Stoics believed that every situation presents an opportunity for growth and improvement. This notion holds particular significance in the context of recovery. Instead of viewing relapse as a failure, we can reframe it as an opportunity to gain insight into our triggers and discover more effective coping strategies. Adopting the Stoic mindset requires us to see challenges as opportunities rather than obstacles. To do so, we must draw upon our wisdom, cultivate courage, and act in alignment with our values. By embracing this perspective, we empower ourselves to navigate the recovery journey with resilience and embrace the transformative potential in every situation.

Mindfulness serves as a foundation for training perceptions. By practicing mindfulness, individuals learn to anchor their attention to the present moment, cultivating a heightened sense of awareness. This practice enables them to observe their thoughts, emotions, and sensations without judgment, fostering a greater understanding of their inner experiences and promoting emotional regulation.

Visualization becomes a powerful tool in training perceptions. By using their imagination, individuals can create mental images of themselves successfully navigating challenging situations. Visualizing positive outcomes cultivates confidence and motivation, enhancing their ability to overcome obstacles and persevere in their recovery journey.

Reframing negative thoughts and perceptions is essential in Stoic Practices for Addiction Recovery. By consciously challenging and replacing negative beliefs, individuals can reinterpret challenges as opportunities for growth. They learn to view setbacks as valuable lessons and stepping stones toward personal development, empowering themselves to find meaning and purpose in their experiences.

Recognizing and challenging cognitive distortions is a vital aspect of training perceptions. Cognitive distortions are irrational and negative thought patterns that can undermine recovery progress. By developing awareness of these distortions, individuals can actively question their validity and replace them with more realistic and constructive thoughts, promoting emotional well-being and resilience.

Cultivating a sense of perspective is a fundamental principle of Stoic practices. By stepping back and taking a broader view of their experiences, individuals avoid getting caught up in negative emotions and gain a more balanced outlook. They recognize that difficulties and setbacks are temporary and part of the human experience, enabling them to navigate challenges with greater resilience and composure.

Take the View From Above

Stoics advocate for periodically adopting a broader perspective on life, often referred to as "Plato's View" (Avalon Malibu, 2020). This practice aligns with the concept of stillness in mindfulness-based therapies. By stepping back and viewing our lives from a higher vantage point, we gain insight into the insignificance of most events and our interconnectedness with humanity. This perspective allows us to recognize the relative smallness of our individual concerns within the grander scheme of things. The practice of viewing from above proves particularly beneficial in group therapy or peer-based recovery models, enabling us to transcend our own worries and extend support to others in need. It fosters a sense of compassion and community as we contribute to the well-being of others while gaining a broader understanding of our place in the world.

Practicing distancing from one's problems involves mentally detaching oneself from the immediate emotions and circumstances surrounding addiction recovery. This method allows individuals to create psychological space and observe their challenges from a more objective standpoint. By stepping outside the situation, they can gain a more comprehensive understanding of their experiences.

Imagining oneself looking down on the situation from a bird's eye view or "Plato's View" is a visualization technique employed in Stoic practices. By visualizing the situation from a higher vantage point, individuals can gain a broader perspective and see their challenges as part of a larger context. This perspective helps them recognize the transient nature of their problems and view them as smaller and less significant in the grand scheme of life.

Considering how problems may seem insignificant in the grand scheme of things helps individuals put their challenges into proper perspective. By recognizing the vastness of the world and the multitude of experiences people face, individuals can gain a sense of humility and realize that their struggles are not unique or insurmountable. This realization can alleviate feelings of overwhelm and instill a sense of resilience.

Recognizing that others have faced similar challenges is a powerful aspect of the Stoic perspective. By acknowledging the shared nature of human experiences, individuals understand that they are not alone in their struggles. This recognition fosters a sense of empathy and connection, allowing individuals to draw strength from the collective wisdom and support of others who have overcome similar obstacles.

By utilizing the practice of taking the view from above, individuals can avoid getting bogged down in negative emotions that can hinder their recovery. By gaining a broader perspective and understanding the transitory nature of challenges, individuals can maintain a sense of calm and detachment. This practice empowers individuals to approach their recovery with a clearer mind, making informed decisions and cultivating emotional resilience.

The Duality of Control

You may be familiar with the Christian serenity prayer that goes, "God, grant me the serenity to accept the things I cannot change, the courage to change the things I can, and wisdom to know the difference" (Avalon Malibu, 2020). This insightful reflection encapsulates the concept of the Dichotomy of Control, which we discussed extensively in Chapter 3 and is applicable to recovery journeys. It acknowledges that there are certain aspects beyond our control, such as the past or the presence of substance abuse or mental health disorder. However, it also emphasizes the power we have to effect change in our lives. In the context of recovery, we focus on what we can change: transforming old habits into healthier ones, shifting our perceptions, and ultimately making positive changes within ourselves. This perspective empowers us to take ownership of our actions and embrace personal growth and transformation on the path to sobriety.

Recognizing the distinction between what is within our control and what is not is the first step in the practice of the Duality of Control. It involves acknowledging that external circumstances, the actions of others, and certain outcomes are beyond our direct influence.

However, we do have control over our thoughts, beliefs, attitudes, choices, and responses to those external factors.

Focusing our energy and attention on the things within our control is a key aspect of the Duality of Control. By directing our efforts towards areas where we can make a difference, such as developing healthy habits, seeking support, engaging in therapy, and making positive choices, we empower ourselves to effect positive change in our recovery journey. This shift in focus helps us channel our energy toward productive and meaningful actions.

Learning to accept and let go of things outside of our control is another crucial element of the Duality of Control. It involves acknowledging that we cannot control every aspect of our recovery or the outcomes we desire. By accepting this reality, we free ourselves from the burden of trying to control the uncontrollable, reducing anxiety and stress. Instead, we learn to adapt, adjust, and find peace in accepting the present moment as it unfolds.

Avoiding becoming overly attached to specific outcomes or expectations is a practice that aligns with the Stoic principle of the Duality of Control. It means releasing rigid attachments to how things should be or how our recovery journey should unfold. By embracing flexibility and adaptability, we open ourselves up to a wider range of possibilities and allow for personal growth and transformation.

By embracing the Duality of Control, individuals can cultivate a sense of inner peace and acceptance. This practice encourages us to focus on what we can control, accept what we cannot, and let go of attachment to specific outcomes. Through this practice, we develop resilience and emotional balance, allowing us to navigate the challenges of addiction recovery with greater equanimity and serenity.

Conclusion

Applying Stoic practices to addiction recovery offers invaluable insights and tools for lasting sobriety. By incorporating these practices, we deepen self-awareness, understand addiction, and develop resilience. Self-reflection helps us identify underlying factors contributing to addiction. Mindfulness allows us to observe thoughts and emotions without judgment. Reframing our perceptions turns setbacks into growth opportunities. Taking the view from above provides perspective and humility. Embracing the duality of control focuses our energy on what we can change. These practices foster personal growth and inner peace.

Chapter 8:

Fostering Emotional

Mastery and Detachment

Emotional sobriety is vital for long-term recovery from addiction. It involves addressing underlying emotional issues, leading to inner peace and well-being. It improves mental health outcomes, boosts self-esteem, and empowers individuals to manage emotions without relying on substances. Emotional sobriety fosters healthy relationships, establishes boundaries, and avoids harmful coping mechanisms. It promotes self-awareness, stress management, and purposeful choices. Stoic techniques such as negative visualization, self-distancing, premeditatio malorum, the dichotomy of control, memento mori, contemplation of the sage, gratitude, the view from above, practicing virtue, and minimalism support emotional mastery and detachment in recovery.

Importance of Emotional Sobriety

Emotional sobriety empowers you to navigate challenges in your daily life without resorting to self-destructive substances (Castle Craig Hospital, 2019). By developing emotional resilience and healthy coping mechanisms, you reduce the risk of relapse and avoid substituting one addiction for another.

The Stoics recognized that a life filled with negative emotions like anger, anxiety, fear, grief, and envy would not lead to a good life (Irvine, 2009). Consequently, they became keen observers of human psychology and emerged as insightful ancient psychologists. They devised methods to prevent the emergence of negative emotions and, if unsuccessful, techniques to extinguish them effectively.

An emotionally sober person embraces a balanced and mature lifestyle, encompassing various important aspects. They possess the ability to effectively manage their emotions and maintain a stable mood, enabling them to navigate both positive and challenging situations with calmness and composure. They approach circumstances with a logical perspective, making rational decisions rather than being overwhelmed by emotions. Resilience is a key trait they possess, allowing them to cope and bounce back even in the face of difficulties. They are self-aware and capable of recognizing and regulating harmful thoughts and behaviors, promoting their mental and emotional well-being. Living in the present moment, they avoid dwelling excessively on the past or worrying excessively about the future. Instead of avoiding problems, they address them directly, demonstrating a proactive approach to life's challenges. They consciously steer clear of self-pity and self-defeating thoughts and behaviors, fostering a positive and empowered mindset. Recognizing the value of human connection, they actively cultivate meaningful relationships and engage with their community. In summary, an emotionally sober person is attuned to their emotions, acknowledges them, and responds to them appropriately, while also being mindful of the tendencies for distraction or repression that may arise.

Benefits of Emotional Sobriety

By fostering emotional mastery and detachment, individuals can address the underlying emotional issues that contribute to addiction, paving the way for sustainable recovery.

One of the key benefits of emotional sobriety is its impact on mental health outcomes. When individuals develop emotional sobriety, they experience improved self-esteem and self-worth. They learn to manage challenging emotions and situations without resorting to substances or addictive behaviors, leading to enhanced mental well-being and a greater sense of inner peace and stability.

Furthermore, emotional sobriety empowers individuals to form healthier relationships with others by developing healthy emotional boundaries. They learn to navigate interpersonal dynamics with clarity and emotional resilience, promoting healthier connections and reducing the likelihood of falling into codependent or enabling patterns. By cultivating emotional sobriety, individuals also avoid replacing addiction with other harmful coping mechanisms, such as excessive work, excessive exercise, or unhealthy relationships.

Emotional sobriety fosters a greater sense of self-awareness and self-acceptance. Through self-reflection and introspection, individuals gain insight into their emotions, triggers, and patterns of behavior. This self-awareness allows them to make conscious choices aligned with their values and goals, and to respond to life's challenges in a more intentional and constructive manner.

Importantly, emotional sobriety has a positive impact on physical health outcomes. Research suggests that individuals with emotional sobriety experience improved immune system function, reduced stress levels, and better overall physical health. By managing emotions effectively and reducing stress, individuals support their immune system, enhance their overall well-being, and reduce the risk of physical health complications.

Lastly, emotional sobriety contributes to a more fulfilling and meaningful life. By cultivating emotional mastery and detachment, individuals develop a greater sense of purpose and connection with others. They are better equipped to navigate life's ups and downs and to find meaning and fulfillment in their relationships, work, and personal pursuits. Emotional sobriety enables individuals to embrace a life of authenticity and genuine connection, fostering a sense of belonging and deepening their overall satisfaction and joy.

Emotional Regulation Skills

Emotional regulation skills refer to the abilities and strategies individuals use to effectively manage and regulate their emotions. These skills play a vital role in maintaining emotional well-being and navigating challenging situations.

Emotion regulation skills are essential for individuals in addiction recovery as they help them cope with negative thoughts and emotions, ultimately aiding in maintaining sobriety (Grace Land Recovery, 2021). These skills require practice and development, as they do not come naturally to human beings from birth.

Managing emotions and emotional responses is a crucial aspect of emotion regulation skills. Babies and children often exhibit temper tantrums due to their limited ability to regulate their emotions. As individuals grow and learn through life experiences, they acquire valuable lessons that improve their ability to deal with negative thoughts and emotions.

Substance misuse hinders emotional growth by numbing negative thoughts and emotions. By relying on substances to cope, individuals with substance use disorders fail to practice and improve their emotion regulation skills. This limitation makes it challenging for them to effectively manage negative thoughts and emotions without turning to substances.

Improving emotion regulation skills is crucial for individuals struggling with substance use because it allows them to better cope with negative thoughts and emotions. Emotion regulation therapy aims to identify, differentiate, and describe emotions, increase acceptance and adaptability, decrease reliance on emotional avoidance strategies, and enhance the ability to utilize emotional information in identifying needs and managing interpersonal relationships.

By achieving these goals of emotion regulation therapy, individuals can learn to use their emotions to their advantage rather than allowing them to control their behavior. Emotion regulation skills enable individuals to identify and accept their emotions, gaining valuable insights into themselves and reducing their reliance on substances as a coping mechanism.

Stoic Techniques to Practice Detachment

The Stoics aimed to eliminate negative emotions rather than eradicating emotions altogether. They understood that our inner goals influence our external actions, and they also recognized that the conscious goals we set for ourselves can significantly impact our emotional well-being in the future (Irvine, 2009).

Detachment involves consciously separating our emotional well-being from external events and circumstances (Schneider, 2023). It entails recognizing that while we cannot control everything that happens to us, we have the power to manage our reactions and responses (remember the Dichotomy of Control?) Detachment does not mean suppressing emotions or becoming indifferent; instead, it emphasizes cultivating a sense of inner resilience and maintaining a balanced perspective in the face of life's ups and downs.

Detachment is related to acceptance because true acceptance involves acknowledging the concrete realities of our lives, even if we are not happy about them. Acceptance in Stoicism involves acknowledging and embracing the realities of our lives (Azide, 2020). It allows us to move beyond repeated anger or frustration over things that exist and empowers us to decide how we will navigate and adapt to the circumstances.

The Stoics exemplified active acceptance of reality. They committed themselves to operate at their highest capacity within the circumstances they faced. Rather than being diminished by their realities, they sought ways to be improved by them. Acceptance opens up space for creative navigation of our next steps and prompts us to ask, "How do I make something of my life? What does my reality require me to do?"

Detachment does not imply a withdrawal from the world or a lack of engagement; rather, it encourages us to engage fully while maintaining emotional autonomy. It involves recognizing that our emotions and inner peace are not solely dependent on external circumstances but are influenced by our interpretation and perception of those circumstances. By practicing detachment, we develop the capacity to maintain our emotional equilibrium even in the midst of adversity, allowing us to respond thoughtfully and effectively.

Through detachment, we cultivate emotional resilience and a greater sense of self-mastery. We become less reactive to external circumstances, allowing us to navigate life's challenges with clarity and composure. Detachment fosters a sense of freedom and inner peace as we release the need for external validation or the constant pursuit of certain outcomes. Instead, we focus on aligning our thoughts, values, and actions with our own sense of purpose and integrity.

Practicing detachment is not an easy endeavor, as it requires consistent effort and self-awareness. It involves recognizing our own attachments, expectations, and fears and consciously working to release their hold on us. By developing a balanced perspective and embracing the inherent uncertainty of life, we open ourselves up to a deeper sense of inner peace and contentment. Here are some Stoic techniques to practice developing this inner calm.

Negative Visualization

This practice involves deliberately envisioning worst-case scenarios, allowing us to mentally prepare for potential challenges. By facing our fears and contemplating potential hardships, we develop the capacity to respond calmly and effectively when adversity strikes. Negative visualization helps us appreciate what we have in the present moment and cultivates gratitude for the things we often take for granted.

Consider a meteorologist who spends her days studying tornadoes without living in constant fear of being killed by one. Similarly, a Stoic can contemplate potential negative events without succumbing to anxiety. Negative visualization doesn't make people gloomy; instead, it enhances their appreciation of the world by preventing them from taking it for granted (Irvine, 2009). Despite occasional negative thoughts, the Stoic can find greater enjoyment in experiences, such as a picnic, fully realizing that such moments might not have happened. This mindset allows them to savor life more deeply than others who avoid such thoughts and take things for granted.

Self-Distancing

By imagining ourselves as objective observers of our own situations, we gain valuable perspective and distance from our emotions. This technique enables us to detach from immediate reactions and view events with greater clarity and objectivity. Self-distancing allows us to make more rational decisions and respond to challenging situations with wisdom and composure.

Premeditatio Malorum

This practice involves anticipating and preparing for potential challenges in advance. By considering what could go wrong, we can develop strategies and contingency plans to mitigate risks and handle difficult situations effectively. Premeditatio malorum allows us to approach life with a proactive mindset, reducing anxiety and increasing our capacity to adapt and overcome obstacles.

Dichotomy of Control

This principle encourages us to focus our attention on what we can control and let go of what is beyond our influence. By recognizing the distinction between external circumstances and our internal responses, we avoid wasting energy on futile concerns. The Dichotomy of Control empowers us to direct our efforts toward the things we can change, such as our attitudes, actions, and values, fostering a sense of inner peace and acceptance.

Momento Mori

This contemplative practice involves reminding ourselves of our own mortality, and acknowledging the finite nature of life. By cultivating an awareness of our impermanence, we gain a sense of urgency and perspective. Memento Mori serves as a powerful reminder to make the most of each moment, to prioritize what truly matters, and to live authentically and purposefully.

Contemplation of the Sage

Reflecting on the lives and teachings of wise individuals from various fields offers valuable insights and guidance for personal growth. By studying the experiences and wisdom of others, we expand our perspectives and learn from their successes and failures. Contemplation of the Sage inspires us to embody virtuous qualities and integrate their teachings into our own lives.

Practice Gratitude

This technique has also come up in earlier chapters of this book. It emphasizes focusing on the present moment and cultivating gratitude for what we have, rather than dwelling on what we lack. By appreciating the blessings and opportunities that surround us, we shift our mindset towards positivity and abundance. Practicing gratitude fosters contentment, resilience, and a greater sense of acceptance.

View From Above

By imagining ourselves from a broader, cosmic perspective, we gain a sense of insignificance in the grand scheme of things. This practice helps us detach from the trivialities and worries of daily life, encouraging us to prioritize what truly matters. Viewing ourselves from a higher vantage point promotes humility, resilience, and a deeper appreciation for the interconnectedness of humanity.

Practice Virtue

Stoicism places great importance on cultivating personal virtue and moral character. Instead of chasing external outcomes or possessions, this practice encourages us to focus on developing qualities such as wisdom, courage, temperance, and justice. By prioritizing virtuous actions, we detach ourselves from external validation and find fulfillment in the pursuit of moral excellence.

Minimalism

Simplifying our lives and reducing attachment to material possessions is a Stoic practice that promotes detachment. By decluttering our physical and mental spaces, we create room for clarity, focus, and serenity. Minimalism encourages us to let go of unnecessary distractions and desires, allowing us to find contentment in simplicity and inner fulfillment.

Conclusion

Emotional mastery and detachment are crucial for achieving emotional sobriety and sustainable recovery. It involves addressing underlying emotional issues to find inner peace and well-being. Emotional sobriety improves mental health outcomes by enhancing self-esteem and enabling the management of challenging emotions without relying on substances. It promotes healthier relationships and the avoidance of harmful coping mechanisms. Cultivating emotional sobriety fosters self-awareness, self-acceptance, and intentional choices aligned with recovery goals. Stoic techniques like negative visualization, self-distancing, premeditatio malorum, the dichotomy of control, memento mori, contemplation of the sage, gratitude, the view from above, practicing virtue, and minimalism provide practical tools for emotional wisdom. By embracing these principles, individuals develop emotional resilience and lead fulfilling lives.

Chapter 9:

Building a Supportive Stoic

Community

Building a supportive Stoic community can be likened to constructing a sturdy and interconnected network of pillars. Each pillar represents an individual Stoic practitioner, contributing their strength and wisdom to the collective structure. Just as the pillars support and reinforce one another, the Stoics in the community provide encouragement, guidance, and understanding to fellow practitioners on their journey toward virtue and tranquility. Together, they form a resilient foundation that withstands life's challenges, fostering growth and resilience for everyone involved.

In our journey of personal growth, finding a supportive community is essential. In this chapter, we explore building connections within a Stoic community and sharing experiences.

Connecting with fellow Stoics enriches our understanding and practice of Stoicism. By establishing connections, we create a network of support and gain valuable insights. We explore ways to foster connections through empathy, kindness, gratitude, humility, and social skills. Cultivating these qualities creates a positive and supportive environment.

Sharing experiences is a powerful means of growth. Finding a receptive audience, being authentic, and focusing on lessons learned are key. Mindful communication, considering timing and feedback, and using storytelling techniques engage listeners. Respecting boundaries and sharing with purpose contribute to the community's well-being.

My Experiences

I have discovered that building a vibrant Stoic community is an exciting journey with various avenues to explore. One effective way is to connect with like-minded individuals who have a genuine interest in Stoic philosophy. Personally, I have actively engaged in Stoic philosophy groups, participated in enlightening discussions on online forums and social media communities dedicated to Stoicism, and attended inspiring Stoic-themed events and workshops. Through these experiences, I have had the pleasure of connecting with passionate individuals who are just as enthusiastic about Stoicism as I am.

Moreover, I have taken the initiative to create regular meetups and study groups, and let me tell you, they have been remarkable in fostering a strong and supportive Stoic community. These gatherings provide a dedicated space where individuals like us can come together, engage in deep conversations about Stoic principles, share personal insights, and provide invaluable support as we apply Stoic practices to our everyday lives. It is truly heartening to witness the sense of belonging and understanding that develops among our community members, resulting in lasting connections and genuine friendships.

Additionally, I have noticed the remarkable growth of online platforms and websites solely focused on Stoicism. These digital spaces serve as invaluable hubs for Stoic enthusiasts like us to connect, share resources, and engage in meaningful discussions. I cannot stress enough how much I have benefited from these online communities, where I have discovered an abundance of enlightening articles, captivating videos, insightful podcasts, and recommended readings. Actively participating in these platforms has not only expanded my understanding of Stoicism but also allowed me to connect with inspiring individuals from around the world, fostering connections that transcend geographical limitations.

By actively seeking like-minded individuals, organizing engaging meetups, and embracing the opportunities provided by online platforms, I have witnessed the incredible growth and development of thriving Stoic communities. These communities create a genuinely nurturing environment for personal growth, shared learning, and the practical exploration of Stoic philosophy. Being part of these communities has enriched my personal journey as a Stoic, providing me with an incredible sense of camaraderie and support on my path toward living a virtuous life. Trust me, you will find immense value and warmth in being part of such a community, where you will be surrounded by fellow travelers who share your enthusiasm and will cheer you every step of the way.

Ways to Establish Connections

From a Stoic perspective, friendship is seen as an integral part of a broader perspective (Chakrapani, 2020). Our innate nature as human beings is to be connected to the larger whole, adopting a cosmopolitan mindset. As a result, we embrace the notion of forgiving the transgressions of others, recognizing them as our fellow brothers and sisters. After all, the transgressions committed by others are external to our own being and have no power to affect us in any significant way. Here are several approaches to forging connections with individuals who embrace Stoic philosophy.

Practice Empathy

Empathy is the ability to understand and share the feelings and experiences of others. In the Stoic community, practicing empathy involves actively seeking to understand others without judgment or criticism. It requires setting aside our own perspectives and biases and genuinely putting ourselves in the shoes of others. By empathizing with others, we create a safe and supportive space where individuals feel heard and understood.

Practice Kindness

Kindness is a fundamental virtue in Stoicism. It involves showing compassion and generosity towards others, even in small ways. Kindness can manifest through acts of service, offering support, or simply being considerate and respectful in our interactions. By practicing kindness, we create a positive and welcoming atmosphere that encourages trust and connection among community members.

Practice Gratitude

Expressing gratitude for others' contributions and positive qualities strengthens the bonds of friendship within most communities. By acknowledging and appreciating the efforts and virtues of others, we foster a sense of recognition and validation. Gratitude also promotes a positive and uplifting environment, where individuals feel valued and encouraged to continue their growth and engagement within the community.

Practice Humility

Humility is essential in establishing connections within the Stoic community. It involves recognizing our own limitations and avoiding arrogance or self-centeredness. Instead, we focus on the value and worth of others. By practicing humility, we create an environment that encourages equality, respect, and open-mindedness. It allows for meaningful interactions and collaborative discussions based on mutual understanding and learning.

Practice Social Skills

Developing strong communication skills, active listening skills, and conflict resolution skills is crucial in establishing connections within the Stoic community. Effective communication ensures that messages are conveyed clearly and respectfully, promoting understanding and reducing misunderstandings. Active listening allows us to genuinely engage with others, making them feel heard and valued. Conflict resolution skills help navigate disagreements and differences of opinion in a constructive and harmonious manner, preserving the unity and cohesion of the community.

Practice Authenticity

Authenticity is the practice of being honest and genuine in our interactions with others. In the Stoic community, being authentic means expressing our true thoughts, feelings, and experiences without pretense or masks. It encourages openness and vulnerability, creating a space where individuals can relate to one another on a deeper level. Authenticity fosters trust and genuine connections, as it allows for the building of meaningful relationships based on shared experiences and understanding.

Practice Vulnerability

Sharing our thoughts and feelings with others in a way that fosters connection and understanding is an act of vulnerability. By being vulnerable, we open ourselves up to the possibility of being seen, heard, and supported by others. It allows for genuine connections to form as individuals relate to and empathize with each other's experiences. Practicing vulnerability in the Stoic community encourages an environment of trust, compassion, and growth.

Practice Forgiveness

Forgiveness is about releasing the grip of past grievances and approaching others with an open mind and heart. Through the practice of forgiveness, we free ourselves from the weight of resentment and make room for understanding and reconciliation. By embracing forgiveness, empathy flourishes, nurturing an environment of compassion and acceptance that strengthens connections and fosters personal growth within the community.

Practice Patience

Patience is a virtue that requires being patient and understanding with others, even in challenging situations. Patience allows for respectful and considerate interactions, even when perspectives differ or conflicts arise. By practicing patience, we create an atmosphere of tolerance and harmony, where individuals feel safe to express themselves and engage in meaningful discussions

Practice Community-Building

Creating opportunities for shared experiences and fostering a sense of belonging and connection among others is vital. This can be achieved by organizing events, workshops, or discussion groups that encourage active participation and collaboration. By building a sense of community, individuals feel supported, inspired, and motivated to continue their growth and engagement within the Stoic philosophy.

Ways to Share Experiences to Foster Growth

By sharing our personal experiences and insights, we can create an environment that cultivates growth and supports ongoing recovery.

Find a Supportive Audience

Seek out individuals or groups who are receptive and empathetic to your experiences. Surrounding yourself with a supportive audience creates a safe and understanding space for sharing and encourages meaningful discussions.

Be Honest and Authentic

Share your experiences with sincerity and without pretense or exaggeration. Being genuine and transparent allows others to connect with your story on a deeper level, promoting authenticity and trust within the community.

Focus on the Positive Aspects

When sharing your experiences, highlight the valuable lessons or personal growth that resulted from them. By emphasizing the positive aspects, you inspire others to find meaning and resilience in their own challenges, fostering growth and learning within the community.

Use Appropriate Language and Tone

Communicate clearly and respectfully, using language and tone that is appropriate for your audience. Consider the sensitivity and needs of your listeners, ensuring that your message is delivered in a way that promotes understanding and empathy.

Be Mindful of Timing

Choose an appropriate time and place to share your experiences. Timing is crucial, as it allows for a receptive and engaged audience. Consider the context and environment in which you are sharing, ensuring that it is conducive to meaningful and focused discussions.

Be Open to Feedback

When sharing your experiences, be open to receiving feedback from others. Listen to their perspectives and insights without becoming defensive or dismissive. Embracing feedback promotes a culture of learning and growth within the community.

Practice Active Listening

Engage in active listening when others share their own experiences with you. Pay attention to their stories, validate their emotions, and ask thoughtful questions. Active listening fosters connection and empathy, creating a supportive and inclusive atmosphere.

Use Storytelling Techniques

Employ storytelling techniques to engage and captivate your audience. Craft your narrative in a way that resonates with others, using compelling anecdotes, vivid descriptions, and relatable examples. Storytelling has the power to inspire, educate, and evoke emotions, leading to deeper connections and shared understanding.

Avoid Oversharing

Be mindful of boundaries and avoid oversharing personal details that may make others uncomfortable. Respect the privacy and sensitivity of others while maintaining a balance between openness and appropriate self-disclosure.

Share With a Purpose

Before sharing your experiences, consider why you want to do so and what you hope to achieve. Reflect on the impact you aim to make within the community and how your story can contribute to the growth, support, and well-being of others.

Conclusion

Building a supportive Stoic community offers opportunities for personal growth, connections, and support. Seeking like-minded individuals, engaging in meetups, and using online platforms create a nurturing environment for exploring Stoic principles, sharing experiences, and forming friendships. Through empathy, kindness, gratitude, humility, and social skills, we foster understanding and acceptance. Sharing experiences inspires others and promotes personal growth. The support of a Stoic community is especially valuable during addiction recovery. By coming together, we create a network of support, friendship, and shared wisdom, empowering us to live virtuous lives and fostering growth and compassion. Let us embrace the opportunities to connect, share, and learn within the Stoic community, knowing we are not alone on this transformative journey.

Conclusion:

Achieving Lasting Sobriety

Through Stoicism

In this book, we have explored the transformative power of Stoic philosophy in the context of achieving sobriety and addiction recovery. By embracing Stoic principles and practicing mindfulness, we have discovered a path to resilience, self-awareness, and personal growth. Throughout our journey, we have examined various aspects of Stoicism and how they can be applied to the challenges of addiction and recovery.

In the introduction, we laid the foundation for understanding Stoic philosophy and its relevance to sobriety. We learned about the nine principles of Stoic philosophy, including embracing natural and rational living, nurturing virtues, and letting go of material attachments. These principles have guided us in our pursuit of a more meaningful and fulfilling life.

In Chapter 2, we explored addiction through the lens of Stoic philosophy. We gained a deeper understanding of the causes and types of addiction, recognizing the interplay between external factors and our internal disposition. By examining addiction from a Stoic perspective, we have cultivated a greater sense of self-awareness and responsibility in our recovery journey.

Chapter 3 focused on embracing the dichotomy of control, a central concept in Stoicism. We learned to focus on what is within our control and accept what is beyond our control. By letting go of attachments to external things and cultivating an inner sense of well-being, we have found resilience and peace amidst the challenges of addiction recovery.

Cultivating resilience through adversity was the theme of Chapter 4. We explored Stoic principles for building mental and emotional resilience, including accepting difficult emotions, developing emotional intelligence, and viewing challenges as opportunities for growth. Through the practice of self-discipline, reframing perspectives, and staying present in the moment, we have nurtured our inner strength and endurance.

Chapter 5 introduced us to the practices of mindfulness and self-awareness. We examined trigger responses and learned to cultivate self-awareness through daily reflection, mindful observation of thoughts and emotions, and active listening. By practicing self-awareness and mindfulness, we have gained insights into our behaviors, thoughts, and emotional patterns, paving the way for personal growth and change.

In Chapter 6, we explored the cultivation of virtue and personal growth in alignment with Stoic philosophy. By embracing difficulties, emulating heroes, reading and practicing Stoic teachings, and appreciating what we have, we have fostered virtuous qualities within ourselves. These virtues, including wisdom, courage, temperance, and justice, have guided us on the path to becoming our ideal selves.

Seeking wisdom through reflection and learning was the focus of Chapter 7. We engaged in self-reflection, identified triggers and high-risk situations, sought support from professionals and support groups, and challenged negative beliefs about addiction and recovery. By understanding ourselves and addiction from a Stoic perspective, we have gained clarity and direction on our recovery journey.

Chapter 8 delved into fostering emotional mastery and detachment. We explored the importance of emotional sobriety and learned Stoic techniques to practice detachment, such as negative visualization, self-distancing, and the contemplation of the sage. By practicing gratitude, adopting a broader perspective, and practicing virtue, we have cultivated emotional resilience and freedom.

In Chapter 9, we recognized the significance of building a supportive Stoic community. We have shared experiences and insights, practiced empathy, kindness, gratitude, and forgiveness, and created opportunities for shared experiences and connections. By actively participating in a Stoic community, we have found companionship, encouragement, and inspiration on our journey to sobriety.

Achieving lasting sobriety through Stoicism is a continuous journey of self-discovery. Stoic philosophy can play a crucial role in maintaining sobriety by providing a guiding framework for self-awareness, resilience, and personal growth. By embracing Stoic principles, individuals are empowered to navigate the challenges of recovery with strength and determination. The practice of mindfulness, emotional mastery, and embracing the Dichotomy of Control enables individuals to remain focused on their journey to sobriety and find fulfillment in the present moment. It encourages continued practice and growth, reminding individuals that the path to a sober and fulfilling life is an ongoing process that requires dedication and perseverance. By incorporating Stoic philosophy into your daily life, you can find the strength and wisdom to overcome obstacles, maintain sobriety, and create a life filled with purpose and contentment.

May you continue to embrace the wisdom of Stoicism, develop resilience, and cultivate self-awareness in your journey towards lasting sobriety. Remember that you are not alone, and by practicing the principles and teachings of Stoicism, you can achieve profound transformation and embrace a life of meaning, purpose, and sobriety.

As we conclude this book, let me leave you with the image of the journey of achieving sobriety through Stoicism as a voyage across the sea of life. In this vast ocean, Stoic philosophy serves as our guiding star, offering us direction and purpose. Just like skilled sailors, we have learned to navigate the tumultuous waters of addiction recovery, steering away from the treacherous whirlpools of negative emotions.

Throughout our voyage, we have erected a powerful lighthouse of self-awareness, shining its light on the hidden depths of our souls. By understanding the causes and triggers of addiction, we have charted a course towards resilience and inner strength.

As we sail, we encounter the winds of challenges and the waves of temptation. Yet, with Stoic principles as our anchor, we remain steadfast, embracing the Dichotomy of Control, knowing that only our inner attitudes are truly within our grasp.

In the company of our fellow sailors, our Stoic community, we find comfort and camaraderie. We share our stories, empathize with one another, and celebrate the victories achieved through virtue and self-improvement. Together, we create a fortified harbor of support, encouraging each other to stay the course and weather any storm that comes our way.

As we sail onward, we raise the sails of mindfulness, constantly attuned to the present moment. By practicing emotional mastery and detachment, we are better equipped to face the turbulent waters, free from the shackles of destructive attachments.

And when we encounter uncharted territories, we rely on the wisdom of Stoic teachings and the guidance of our virtuous heroes. They serve as beacons of inspiration, illuminating the path towards our ideal selves.

As we continue our journey, we must never forget that our voyage to sobriety is not a solitary endeavor. We are not lone sailors in this vast ocean, but part of a united fleet, each vessel supporting and propelling one another towards the shores of fulfillment and lasting sobriety.

May the Stoic winds of wisdom and resilience carry us forward, as we sail towards a life of purpose, contentment, and triumph over addiction. As the horizon beckons, let us embrace the Stoic compass of virtue and self-awareness, guiding us through the ever-changing tides of life. With Stoicism as our constant companion, we can navigate this transformative journey with courage, finding solace in the journey itself, and celebrating the beautiful moments that unfold along the way.

References

Ackerman, C. E. (2020, April 1). *What is self-awareness? (+5 Ways to Be More Self-Aware).* Positive Psychology. https://positivepsychology.com/self-awareness-matters-how-you-can-be-more-self-aware/#theory

Aurelius, M. (2017a). *Marcus Aurelius, Meditations 2.17.* Lexundria. https://lexundria.com/m_aur_med/2.17/lg#:~:text=And%2C%20to%20say%20all%20in

Aurelius, M. (2017b). *Marcus Aurelius, Meditations 5.20* (G. Long, Ed.). Lexundria. https://lexundria.com/m_aur_med/5.20/lg

Avalon Malibu. (2020, October 6). *Finding strength in recovery through stoicism.* Avalon Malibu. https://www.avalonmalibu.com/blog/finding-strength-in-recovery-through-stoicism/

Azide, E. (2020, May 30). *The philosophy of acceptance.* The Philosophy of Everything. https://www.thephilosophyofeverything.com/blog/the-philosophy-of-acceptance

Baines, S. (2020, November 10). *9 principles of stoicism which will improve your life.* Medium. https://stephenbaines.medium.com/9-

principles-of-stoicism-which-will-improve-your-life-6ca089c8eb37

Baldwin, S., & Bick, D. (2017). First-time fathers' needs and experiences of transition to fatherhood in relation to their mental health and wellbeing. *JBI Database of Systematic Reviews and Implementation Reports*, *15*(3), 647–656. https://doi.org/10.11124/jbisrir-2016-003031

Bettridge, N. (2023, March 10). *The links between stoicism and growth mindset.* LinkedIn. https://www.linkedin.com/pulse/links-between-stoicism-growth-mindset-neela-bettridge

Camilleri, A. (2023, April 18). *Stoicism: Nature and the problem of evil.* PhilosophyMT. https://philosophymt.com/stoicism-nature-and-the-problem-of-evil/

Castle Craig Hospital. (2019, July 23). *Emotional sobriety: The key to addiction recovery.* Castle Craig Hospital. https://www.castlecraig.co.uk/addiction/emotional-sobriety-addiction-recovery/#:~:text=Emotional%20sobriety%20helps%20you%20deal

Chakrapani, C. (2020, September). *Stoicism and the art of friendship.* The Stoic Gym. https://thestoicgym.com/the-stoic-magazine/article/177

Cherry, K. (2023, March 10). *What is self-awareness?* Verywell Mind.

https://www.verywellmind.com/what-is-self-awareness-2795023

Chew, L. (2018, March 1). *9 Stoic practices that will help you thrive in the madness of modernity*. Daily Stoic. https://dailystoic.com/stoicism-modernity/

Cloos, Christopher. (2019, February 17). *When the obstacle becomes the way forward — Marcus Aurelius' meditations 5.20*. The Philosophical Life. https://christophercloos.com/the-obstacle-becomes-the-way/#:~:text=The%20quote%20from%20Marcus%20Aurelius

Cleveland Clinic. (2022, March 22). *21 ways to practice mindfulness*. Cleveland Clinic. https://health.clevelandclinic.org/what-is-mindfulness/

Cleveland Clinic. (2023, March 16). *Addiction*. Cleveland Clinic. https://my.clevelandclinic.org/health/diseases/6407-addiction

Cooks-Campbell, A. (2022, July 15). *Triggers: Learn to recognize and deal with them*. BetterUp. https://www.betterup.com/blog/triggers

Daily Stoic. (2019, June 26). *The highest good: An introduction to the 4 Stoic virtues*. Daily Stoic. https://dailystoic.com/4-stoic-virtues/

Daily Stoic. (2020, January 2). *7 Stoic practices to help you become your ideal self in 2020*. Daily Stoic.

https://dailystoic.com/7-stoic-practices-to-help-you-become-your-ideal-self-in-2020/

Ergil, L. Y. (2021, July 29). *Stoic life lessons: The latest in self-development.* Daily Sabah. https://www.dailysabah.com/life/stoic-life-lessons-the-latest-in-self-development/news

FitMind. (2020, July 1). *Stoicism: A durable mindset.* FitMind. https://fitmind.com/blog-collection/stoic-mindset

Garrett, J. (2021, September 10). *What is Stoicism? Explained in 3 Beliefs.* TheCollector. https://www.thecollector.com/what-is-stoicism-the-stoics-beliefs/

Gellius, A. (1927). *Aulus Gellius, Attic nights, Book XIX, I, section arg* (J. C. Rolfe, Ed.). Perseus Digital Library. http://www.perseus.tufts.edu/hopper/text?doc=Perseus%3Atext%3A2007.01.0072%3Abook%3D19%3Achapter%3D1%3Asection%3D1arg

Gill, N. S. (2019). *Does the serenity prayer echo the Greco-Roman notion of Stoicism?* ThoughtCo. https://www.thoughtco.com/stoics-and-moral-philosophy-4068536

Grace Land Recovery. (2021, May 7). *The importance of emotion regulation skills in addiction recovery.* Grace Land Recovery. https://www.gracelandrecovery.com/blog/202

1/may/the-importance-of-emotion-regulation-skills-in-a/

Hanselman, S. (2016, October 20). *Self-awareness and emotional intelligence: The keys to your best self.* Daily Stoic. https://dailystoic.com/self-awareness-and-emotional-intelligence-the-keys-to-your-best-self/

Hanselman, S. (2020, October 3). *The 9 core Stoic beliefs.* Daily Stoic. https://dailystoic.com/9-core-stoic-beliefs/

Haselhuhn, S. (2018, March 26). *How to develop Stoic mental toughness and resilience: Interview with coach Seth Haselhuhn.* Daily Stoic. https://dailystoic.com/seth-haselhuhn/

iPerceptive. (n.d.). *Stoic quotes on virtue - iPerceptive.* Iperceptive.com. https://iperceptive.com/quotes/stoicism-virtue.html

Irvine, W. B. (2009). *A guide to the good life: The ancient art of Stoic joy.* Oxford University Press.

McLane, A. (2020, April 8). *How the Stoics thrive in adversity.* Fulfilling Strategy. https://fulfillingstrategy.com/stoicsthriveinadversity/#:~:text=The%20Stoics%20teach%20us%20that

National Institute on Drug Abuse. (2018, June). *Understanding drug use and addiction drug facts.* National Institute on Drug Abuse.

https://nida.nih.gov/publications/drugfacts/understanding-drug-use-addiction

Quantumplatonics. (2015, November 11). *Stoicism & marijuana.* Philosophy in Seconds. https://philosophyinseconds.wordpress.com/2015/11/11/43-stoicism-marijuana/#:~:text=The%20Stoics%20believed%20that%20one

Richmond, A. (2021, January 20). *How to reflect on your day like a Stoic.* Stoicism—Philosophy as a Way of Life. https://medium.com/stoicism-philosophy-as-a-way-of-life/how-to-reflect-on-your-day-like-a-stoic-dfe9bf639b63#:~:text=The%20timeless%20value%20of%20the%20Stoic%20practice%20of%20daily%20reflection.&text=The%20Stoics%20believed%20in%20continually

Robertson, D. J. (2020, April 13). *Stoicism and psychological resilience.* Medium. https://medium.com/stoicism-philosophy-as-a-way-of-life/stoicism-and-psychological-resilience-12e3917563e3

Robertson, D. J. (2022, August 2). *How Stoicism could help you build resilience.* Psychology Today. https://www.psychologytoday.com/intl/blog/the-psychology-stoicism/202208/how-stoicism-could-help-you-build-resilience

Schneider, T. (2023, April 11). *Inner calm, outer success: Practicing Stoic techniques for inner calm - Detachment.* LinkedIn.

https://www.linkedin.com/pulse/inner-calm-outer-success-practicing-stoic-techniques-schneider-1e#:~:text=In%20Stoicism%2C%20detachment%20is%20about

Seddon, K. H. (n.d.). *Epictetus.* Internet Encyclopedia of Philosophy. https://iep.utm.edu/epictetu/

Seneca. (n.d.). *On the faults of the spirit, by Seneca* (R. M. Gummere, Ed.). Monadnock Valley Press. https://monadnock.net/seneca/53.html

Tallon, M. (2020, April 13). *10 simple ways to practice mindfulness in our daily life.* Monique Tallon. https://moniquetallon.com/10-simple-ways-to-practice-mindfulness-in-our-daily-life/

The Phoenix Recovery Center. (2020, October 30). *The root causes of addiction.* The Phoenix Recovery Center. https://www.thephoenixrc.com/root-cause-of-addiction/#:~:text=The%20root%20causes%20of%20addiction%20include%20trauma%2C%20mental%20health%20struggles

The Skills Development Scotland. (n.d.). *How to learn from your past experiences.* The Skills Development Scotland. https://careers.myworldofwork.co.uk/career-advice/building-confidence/how-to-learn-from-your-past-experiences#:~:text=Enhancing%20your%20ability%20to%20reflect

Tosin. (2023a, January 16). *Wealth and wisdom: Do Stoics care about money?* The Insignificant Soul. https://thebeautyinbeinginsignificant.com/stoic s-money/

Tosin. (2023b, February 8). *Unlock self-control: Did the Stoics drink alcohol?* The Insignificant Soul. https://thebeautyinbeinginsignificant.com/stoic s-drink- alcohol/#:~:text=In%20Stoicism%2C%20exce ssive%20alcohol%20consumption

Vecchiola, B. (2022a, September 22). *Stoic recovery, 1: How can Stoic philosophy help me recovery from addiction?* LinkedIn. https://www.linkedin.com/pulse/stoic- recovery-1-how-can-philosophy-help-me-from- brandon-vecchiola

Vecchiola, B. (2022b, September 29). *Stoic recovery, 2: What is the dichotomy of control?* LinkedIn. https://www.linkedin.com/pulse/stoic- recovery-2-what-dichotomy-control-brandon- vecchiola

Weaver, T. (2019a, October 17). *The 4 Stoic virtues.* Orion Philosophy. https://www.orionphilosophy.com/stoic- blog/4-stoic-virtues

Weaver, T. (2019b, November 4). *Stoicism & the dichotomy of control.* Orion Philosophy. https://www.orionphilosophy.com/stoic- blog/stoicism-and-the-dichotomy-of-control

Weaver, T. (2022, July 21). *Stoicism & control.* Orion
    Philosophy.
    https://www.orionphilosophy.com/stoic-
    blog/stoicism-control

Ye, B. (2019, December 1). *Stoicism: How to manage the
    difficulties   of   life.*   The   Startup.
    https://medium.com/swlh/stoicism-how-to-
    manage-the-difficulties-of-life-c015e2dff07b

Made in the USA
Las Vegas, NV
11 September 2023

77427670R10105